A
GEOGRAPHIC DICTIONARY OF CONNECTICUT AND RHODE ISLAND

By
HENRY GANNETT

Two Volumes in One

Baltimore
GENEALOGICAL PUBLISHING CO., INC.
1978

Originally published: Washington, D.C., 1894
as *A Geographic Dictionary of Connecticut,*
U.S. Geological Survey, Bulletin No. 117
and *A Geographic Dictionary of Rhode Island,*
U.S. Geological Survey, Bulletin No. 115
Reprinted: Two volumes in one
Genealogical Publishing Co., Inc.
Baltimore, 1978
From a volume in the Enoch Pratt Free Library
Baltimore, Maryland
Library of Congress Catalogue Card Number 78-59123
International Standard Book Number 0-8063-0820-6

UNITED STATES GEOLOGICAL SURVEY

J. W. POWELL, DIRECTOR

A

GEOGRAPHIC DICTIONARY

OF

CONNECTICUT

BY

HENRY GANNETT

WASHINGTON

GOVERNMENT PRINTING OFFICE

1894

LETTER OF TRANSMITTAL.

DEPARTMENT OF THE INTERIOR,
U. S. GEOLOGICAL SURVEY,
DIVISION OF GEOGRAPHY,
Washington, D. C., February 1, 1894.

SIR: I have the honor to transmit herewith for publication a geographic dictionary of Connecticut.

Very respectfully,

HENRY GANNETT,
Chief Topographer.

Hon. J. W. POWELL,
Director U. S. Geological Survey.

A GEOGRAPHIC DICTIONARY OF CONNECTICUT.

By Henry Gannett.

The Geographic Dictionary of Connecticut, which constitutes this bulletin, is designed to aid in finding any geographic feature upon the atlas sheets of that State published by the U. S. Geological Survey. It contains all the names given upon those sheets, and no other. Under each name is a brief statement of the character and locality of the feature, and opposite is the name of the atlas sheet or sheets upon which it is to be found.

The atlas sheets upon which the State is represented are the result of a survey made at the joint expense of the U. S. Geological Survey and the State of Connecticut. The scale upon which the sheets are published is 1:62500; that is, a distance of 62,500 inches upon the ground, or very nearly 1 mile, is represented by 1 inch upon the map. Relief, or the variation of elevation, is represented by contour lines or lines of equal elevation above mean sea level, these contour lines being at vertical intervals of 20 feet; so that each contour indicates a level 20 feet higher than the one below it. Upon the map all water bodies, that is, bays, ponds, rivers, etc., are represented in blue; the contour lines representing the relief, together with the figures showing elevation; are printed in brown; and the lettering and all symbols of the works of man are printed in black.

The area of the State is represented upon 33 sheets, each sheet comprising 15 minutes of latitude by 15 minutes of longitude. Each sheet, therefore, includes about 17½ miles from north to south, and about 13 miles from east to west. Of these sheets only 20 lie entirely or practically within the State; the others include portions of the adjacent States of Rhode Island, Massachusetts, and New York. The following is a list of the sheets showing the names assigned to them and their limits in latitude and longitude:

7

Sheets.	Limits.			
	In latitude.		In longitude.	
	° ′	° ′	° ′	° ′
Sheffield	42 00 to	42 15	73 15 to	73 30
Sandisfield	42 00	42 15	73 00	73 15
Granville................	42 00	42 15	72 30	73 00
Springfield	42 00	42 15	72 15	72 30
Palmer..................	42 00	42 15	72 00	72 15
Brookfield..............	42 00	42 15	71 45	72 00
Webster	42 00	42 15	71 30	71 45
Cornwall...............	41 45	42 00	73 15	73 30
Winsted................	41 45	42 00	73 00	73 15
Granby	41 45	42 00	72 30	73 00
Hartford	41 45	42 00	72 15	72 30
Tolland	41 45	42 00	72 00	72 15
Woodstock	41 45	42 00	71 45	72 00
Putnam.................	41 45	42 00	71 30	71 45
Clove	41 30	41 45	73 30	73 45
New Milford............	41 30	41 45	73 15	73 30
Waterbury	41 30	41 45	73 00	73 15
Meriden................	41 30	41 45	72 30	73 00
Middletown	41 30	41 45	72 15	72 30
Gilead	41 30	41 45	72 00	72 15
Norwich................	41 30	41 45	71 45	72 00
Moosup	41 30	41 45	71 30	71 45
Carmel.................	41 15	41 30	73 30	73 45
Danbury	41 15	41 30	73 15	73 30
Derby..................	41 15	41 30	73 00	73 15
New Haven.............	41 15	41 30	72 30	73 00
Guilford................	41 15	41 30	72 15	72 30
Saybrook...............	41 15	41 30	72 15	72 30
New London............	41 15	41 30	71 45	72 00
Stonington	41 15	41 30	71 30	71 45
Stamford...............	41 00	41 15	73 30	73 45
Norwalk	41 00	41 15	73 15	73 30
Bridgeport	41 00	41 15	73 00	73 15

The spelling of the names conforms to the decisions of the U. S. Board on Geographic Names.

Connecticut is one of the original 13 States; it ratified the Constitution on January 9, 1788.

The boundary lines between Rhode Island on the one hand and Massachusetts and Connecticut on the other are extremely irregular, having originated with early colonial charters, and having been modified subsequently by conventions and agreements, so that it is impossible to describe them in any other way than by representing them upon a map or by a detailed statement of courses and distances.

The total area of the State is 4,990 square miles. Of this area 145 square miles are water surface, consisting of bays, ponds, rivers, etc., which, deducted from the total area, leaves 4,845 square miles of land surface.

The State is divided into eight counties, with land areas as follows:

County.	Square miles.
Fairfield	675
Hartford	751
Litchfield	914
Middlesex	381
New Haven	638
New London	670
Tolland	407
Windham	554

A GEOGRAPHIC DICTIONARY OF CONNECTICUT.

Names of sheets.

Abington; village in Pomfret .... Woodstock.

Above All; hill in southwest part of Warren; elevation, 1,456 feet .. New Milford.

Alewife; cove extending from Long Island Sound into southern coast of Waterford and New London.................................... New London.

Alexander; pond in northwest part of Killingly .... Putnam.

Allen; hill in eastern part of Brooklyn; elevation, 340 feet.......... Putnam.

Allen; hill in Pomfret... Woodstock.

Allison; pond in southern part of Killingworth..................... Guilford.

Allyn Point; village in western part of Ledyard, on Thames River; and on Norwich and Worcester R. R.............................. New London.

Almyville; village in central part of Plainfield, on Moosup River; and on Providence division New York and New England R. R........ Moosup.

Alworth; hill on northwest part of Brooklyn; elevation, 749 feet.... Woodstock.

Amos; lake in eastern part of Preston.............................. Moosup.

Andover; town in southern part of Tolland County; area, 13 square { Tolland.
miles... { Gilead.

Andover; village in central part of Andover, on Hop River; and on Hop River branch New York and New England R. R............. Gilead.

Andrew; pond in western part of Danbury......................... Carmel.

Andrew; hill in southwest part of Naugatuck; elevation, 700 feet... Derby.

Angusville; brook rising in southern part of North Stonington, flowing south into Stonington, and empties into Wequetequock...... Stonington.

Ansonia; town in western part of New Haven County; area, 6 square miles... Derby.

Ansonia; borough and principal place of Ansonia, situated in central part of town, on Naugatuck River; and on Naugatuck division New York and New England R. R............................... Derby.

Archer; mountain in central part of Lyme; altitude, 368 feet........ Saybrook.

Arnold; village in eastern part of Haddam, on Connecticut River; and on Connecticut Valley division New York, New Haven and Hartford R. R... Guilford.

Ash; brook rising in western part of Coventry, tributary to Skungamaug River.. Tolland.

Ash; creek in southeast part of Fairfield, tributary to Rooster River. Bridgeport.

Ashford; town in western part of Windham County; area, 23 square miles .... Woodstock.

Ashford; village in town of same name............................. Woodstock.

Ashland; pond in northwest part of Griswold .... Moosup.

Aspetuck; village in Easton .... Norwalk.

Aspetuck; river rising in eastern part of Redding, flows south { Danbury.
through Easton, and empties into Saugatuck River in northern } Norwalk.
part of Westport ....

11

Names of sheets.

Assekonk; brook in southern part North Stonington, tributary to Shunock River.. Stonington.

Assekonk; swamp in southern part North Stonington .. .. Stonington.

Attawaugan; village in northwest part of Killingly, on Fivemile River... Putnam.

Atwoodville; village in Mansfield.. Woodstock.

Auger; pond in western part of Thompson............................ Putnam.

Augerville; village in eastern part of Hamden....................... New Haven.

Avery; pond in southern part of Preston .... Stonington.

Avery; point of land projecting from southwest coast of Groton into Long Island Sound... New London.

Avery; hill in northern part of Franklin; elevation, 540 feet........ Norwich.

Avery; hill in northwest part of Ledyard; elevation, 320 feet .... New London.

Avon; town in western part of Hartford County; area, 23 square miles. Granby.

Avon; principal village in northeast part of town of same name, on New York, New Haven and Hartford R. R., Northampton division .... Granby.

Ayer; hill in northeast part of Ledyard; elevation, 500 feet.......... Stonington.

Babcock; pond in southwest part of Colchester...................... Gilead.

Babes; hill in northern part of Salisbury; elevation, 1,000 feet ...... Sheffield.

Back; river in southwest part of Old Lyme, tributary to Connecticut River .... Saybrook.

Back; river in southern part of Old Saybrook, flowing into Long Island Sound .... Saybrook.

Back; brook in northern part of Portland, tributary to Connecticut River .... Middletown.

Bailey; hill in northwest part of Groton; elevation, 241 feet .... New London.

Bailey; pond in northeastern corner of Voluntown .... Moosup.

Baileyville; village in central part of Middlefield, on Air Line division New York, New Haven and Hartford R. R................. Middletown.

Baker; hill in eastern part of Chatham; elevation, 680 feet.......... Gilead.

Baker; cove extending from Long Island Sound into southwest coast of Groton .... New London.

Bakersville; village in southwest part of New Hartford .... Winsted.

Bald; hill in central part of East Haddam .... Saybrook.

Bald; hill in Union; elevation, 1,286 feet............................. Woodstock.

Bald; hill in central part of Kent; elevation, 1,300 feet .... New Milford.

Bald; hill in northwest part of Coventry; elevation, 944 feet........ Tolland.

Bald; mountain in eastern part of Somers; altitude, 1,120 feet ...... Tolland.

Bald Hill; village in Wilton... Norwalk.

Baldwin; village in western part of Milford, on Housatonic River, and on Naugatuck division New York, New Haven and Hartford R. R. Bridgeport.

Baldwin; hill in southwest part of Ledyard, extending into Groton; elevation, 240 feet.. New London.

Ball; brook in southern part of New Fairfield, tributary to Wood Creek .... { Danbury. / Carmel.

Ball; brook in northern part of Salisbury, tributary to Moore Brook.. Sheffield.

Ball; hill in western part of Mansfield; elevation, 652 feet.......... Tolland.

Ball; mountain in northwest part of Norfolk; altitude, 1,760 feet.... Sandisfield.

Ball; pond in southwest part of New Fairfield .... Carmel.

Ball Pond; village in southwest part of New Fairfield .... Carmel.

Ballouville; village in northern part of Killingly, on Fivemile River.. Putnam.

Ballwall; brook in central part of Easton, tributary to Aspetuck River. Danbury.

Baltic; village in southern part of Sprague, on Shetucket River; also on Providence division New York and New England R. R........ Norwich.

Names of sheets.

Banksville; village in extreme northern part of Greenwich........... Stamford.

Bantam; river rising in southern part of Goshen, flowing southwest through central part of Litchfield and northwest part of Morris, into Shepaug River in northern part of Washington .... Waterbury.

Bantam; lake in northern part of Morris, extending into southern part of Litchfield... Waterbury.

Bantam Falls; village in western part of Litchfield on Bantam River and on Shepaug, Litchfield and Northern R. R .... Waterbury.

Bare; hill in northwest part of Voluntown........................... Moosup.

Barkhamsted; town in northeast part of Litchfield County; area, { Granby. 39 square miles. { Winsted.

Barkhamsted; village in eastern part of town of same name...... Granby.

Barndoor; two hills in southern part of Granby; altitudes, 700 and 600 feet, respectively... Granby.

Barrack; mountain in southwest part of Canaan; altitude, 1,140... Cornwall.

Barses; pond in southeast part of New Fairfield.................... Danbury.

Bartlett; village in northeast part of Waterford.................... New London.

Bartlett Tower; hill in northeast part of Simsbury, extending into Bloomfield; elevation, 560 feet.................................... Granby.

Bashan; lake in central part of East Haddam...................... Saybrook.

Bashon; hill in western part of Bozrah; elevation, 480 feet......... Norwich.

Batcom; pond in southwest part of Norfolk .... Winsted.

Bate; pond in southwest part of Canterbury....................... Norwich.

Battle Swamp; brook rising in southern part of Washington, flowing into Shepaug River in northwest part of Roxbury............ New Milford.

Bay; mountain in southern part of Griswold; altitude 560 feet...... Moosup.

Beach; pond in east central part of Voluntown, extending into Exeter, R. I.. Moosup.

Beacon; hill in southwest part of East Haven; elevation, 160 feet.... New Haven.

Beacon; hill in southwest part of Branford; elevation, 120 feet...... New Haven.

Beacon; hill in northern part of Beacon Falls, and Bethany, extending into Naugatuck; has two peaks, elevation of one being 600 and of the other 700 feet... Derby.

Beacon Falls; town in western part of New Haven County; area, 10 square miles... Derby.

Beacon Falls; village in central part of town of same name on Naugatuck River, also, on Naugatuck division, New York, New Haven and Hartford R. R .... Derby.

Beacon Hill; brook in south and east part of Naugatuck, tributary to Naugatuck River .... Derby.

Bear; hill in northeast part of New Milford; elevation, 1,320 feet.... New Milford.

Bear; hill in central part of Bozrah; elevation, 500 feet.............. Norwich.

Bear; hill in eastern part of Middletown; elevation, 650 feet....... Middletown.

Bear; mountain in northwest part of Salisbury; altitude, 2,355 feet. Sheffield.

Beardsley; pond in northwest part of Sharon .... Cornwall.

Beaslick; brook in southern part of Salisbury, flowing into Wononpakok Lake.. Cornwall.

Beaslick; pond in southern part of Salisbury .... Cornwall.

Beaver; brook rising in western part of Bethel, flowing north into Still River in eastern part of Danbury............................ Danbury.

Beaver; brook rising in northwest part of East Lyme, flowing west into Eight Mile River, in central part of Lyme.................. Saybrook.

Beaver; brook rising in southwest part of Hartland, flowing southeast through Barkhamsted into east branch of Farmington River. Granby.

Beaver; brook, right branch of Saugatuck River, in Weston .... Norwalk.

Names of sheets.

Beaver; brook in Windham and Scotland........................... Norwich.

Beaver; brook rising in eastern part of Franklin, flowing into Shetucket River, in southern part of Sprague...................... Norwich.

Beaver; hill in northern part of New Haven; elevation, 100 feet.... New Haven.

Beaverdam; brook in Eastford,, tributary to Natchaug River....... Woodstock.

Bee; brook rising in southeast part of Warren, flowing south into
Shepaug River, in northern part of Washington.................. New Milford.

Belcher; brook in eastern part of Berlin, tributary to Sebethe River Meriden.

Beldon; hill in Wilton... Norwalk.

Belle; island off coast of Norwalk................................... Norwalk.

Benedict; pond in northeast part of Norfolk................. .... Sandisfield.

Bennett; two small ponds in northern part of Ridgefield............. Danbury.

Bennett Bridge; village in southern part of Southbury on Pompe- ⎱ Danbury.
raug and Housatonic Rivers..................................... ⎰ Derby.

Berkshire; village in eastern part of Newtown .... Danbury.

Berkshire Mill; pond in west central part of Bridgeport............. Bridgeport.

Berlin; town in southwest part of Hartford County; area, 28 square ⎱ Meriden.
miles. ⎰ Middletown.

Berlin; village in northern part of town of same name on New York ⎧
and New England R. R. also on New York, New Haven and Hart- ⎬ Middletown.
ford R. R .... ⎩ Meriden.

Beseck; mountain in western part of Middlefield and extending in ⎱ Guilford.
eastern part of Wattingford, greatest elevation being 840 feet .. ⎰ Middletown.

Beseck; lake in southwest part of Middlefield...................... Middletown.

Bethany; town in western part of New Haven County; area, 21 square ⎱ Derby.
miles. ⎰ New Haven.

Bethany; village in central part of town of same name.............. New Haven.

Bethel; town in northern part of Fairfield County; area, 16 square
miles .... Danbury.

Bethel; borough in town of same name situated in western part of
town on Danbury and Norwalk division, Housatonic R. R....... Danbury.

Bethlehem; town in southern part of Litchfield County; area, 19 ⎱ New Milford.
square miles. ⎰ Waterbury.

Bethlehem; village in central part of town of same name .... Waterbury.

Bett; island near the Norwalk islands off mouth of Norwalk River
and Long Island Sound .... Norwalk.

Big Meadow, pond in northwest part of Watertown................ Waterbury.

Bigelow; brook rising in Union, forming northwestern boundary line
between Ashford and Eastford and thence flowing into Natchaug
River... Woodstock

Bill Hill; village in southwest part of Lyme........................ Saybrook.

Billings; lake in northern part of North Stonington .... Moosup.

Bingham; pond in northwest part of Salisbury...................... Sheffield.

Birge; pond in central part of Bristol .... Meriden.

Birmingham; borough in central part of Derby at junction of Nau-
gatuck and Housatonic rivers; also on Naugatuck division, New
York, New Haven and Hartford R. R., and New Haven and Derby
R. R .... Derby.

Bissel; ferry in eastern part of Windsor .... Hartford.

Black; brook in northwest part of Woodbridge, tributary to Bladens
River.. Derby.

Black; pond in Woodstock .... Woodstock.

Black; pond on boundary line between Meriden and Middlefield .... Middletown.

Black Point; village on extreme southern point of East Lyme, on
Long Island Sound... New London.

Names of sheets.

Black Rock; village in southwest part of Bridgeport on Long Island
Sound... Bridgeport.

Black Rock; harbor; arm of Long Island Sound, indenting southwest
coast of Bridgeport.. Bridgeport.

Blackhall; pond in northeast part of Old Lyme...................... Saybrook.

Blackhall; village in southwest part of Old Lyme, on Shore Line
division New York, New Haven and Hartford R. R................ Saybrook.

Blackhall; river rising in northeast part of Old Lyme, flowing southwest into Long Island Sound...................................... Saybrook.

Blackberry; river rising in Norfolk, flowing west into Housatonic
River in west central part of North Canaan...................... Sheffield.

Blackstone Rocks; group of islands off southern coast of Branford,
in Long Island Sound.. New Haven.

Blackwell; brook rising in southern part of Pomfret, flowing southeast into Quinebaug River in northeast part of Canterbury ...... Putnam.

Bladen; river rising in North Woodbridge, flowing west into Naugatuck River, in central part of Seymour........................... Derby.

Blake; hill in western part of Windham; elevation, 500 feet......... Norwich.

Blakely; pond in eastern part of Norfolk .... Winsted.

Blockledge; river rising in Bolton, flowing south through Hebron
and Marlboro into Salmon River in western part of Colchester.... Gilead.

Bloomfield; town in central part of Hartford County; area, 28 square ⎰ Granby.
miles.   ⎱ Hartford.

Bloomfield; village in eastern part of town of same name on Central
New England and Western R. R.................................... Hartford.

Blue; hill in Franklin and Bozrah; elevation, 500 feet.............. Norwich.

Bluff; point of land projecting from southern coast of Groton into
Long Island Sound.. New London.

Bluff Head; hill in northern part of Guilford; elevation, 765 feet..... Guilford.

Boardman Bridge; village in western part of New Milford, on Housatonic River, also on Housatonic R. R .... New Milford.

Bog Meadow; pond in central part of Sharon....................... Cornwall.

Boggs; pond in northwest part of Danbury......................... Carmel.

Bolton; town in western part of Tolland County; area, 19 square ⎰ Tolland.
miles.   ⎱ Gilead.

Bolton; village in central part of town of same name.............. Tolland.

Bolton Notch; village in northern part of Bolton.................. Tolland.

Booth; hill in northeast part of Trumbull and in Huntington; elevation, 530 feet.. Derby.

Botsford; village in southeast part of Newtown, on Housatonic R. R.. Danbury.

Bower: hill in southwest part of Oxford, having two peaks, the altitude of one being 400 feet and that of the other 440 feet......... Derby.

Box; mountain in northwest part of Bolton and in Vernon; altitude,
870 feet... Tolland.

Boyle; brook in northern part of East Hartford, tributary to Connecticut River.. Hartford.

Boys Halfway; river rising in eastern Monroe, flowing north into
Housatonic River... Derby.

Bozrah; town in western part of New London County; area, 20 square
miles .... Norwich.

Bozrah Street; village in central part of Bozrah .... Norwich.

Bozrahville; village in northwest part of Bozrah, on Yantic River.. Norwich.

Bradford; mountain in northeast part of Canaan; altitude, 1,927 feet. Cornwall.

Branchville; village in southeast part of Ridgefield, on Norwalk
River; also on Housatonic R. R.................................. Danbury.

Names of sheets.

Brandy; hill in western part of Torrington; elevation, 1,160 feet... Winsted.

Branford; town in southern part of New Haven County; area, 23 { New Haven.
square miles.   { Guilford.

Branford; village in central part of town of same name, on Branford
River, also on Shore Line division New York, New Haven and
Hartford R. R... New Haven.

Branford; point projecting from southwest coast of Branford into
Branford Harbor... New Haven.

Branford; river rising in western part of Guilford, flowing southwest
through North Branford and Branford, into Long Island Sound .. New Haven.

Branford; harbor, arm of Long Island Sound, indenting southern
coast of Branford.. New Haven.

Breakneck; hill in northern part of Middlebury; elevation, 829 feet. Waterbury.

Breakneck; hill in north central part of Killingly; elevation, 640
feet .... Putnam.

Breakneck; pond in northeast part of Union....................... Brookfield.

Brewster; pond in western part of Lebanon....................... Gilead.

Bride; lake in southwest part of East Lyme .... New London.

Bride Lake; brook in southwest part of East Lyme, flowing into Long
Island Sound.. New London.

Bridgeport; town in southeast part of Fairfield County; area, 9
square miles .... Bridgeport.

Bridgewater; town in southern part of Litchfield County; area, 15 { New Milford.
square miles.   { Danbury.

Bridgewater; village in central part of town of same name......... New Milford.

Briggs; hill in southern part of Sherman; elevation, 1,060 feet...... New Milford.

Brightview; village in southwest part of East Haven .... New Haven.

Bristol; town in southwestern part of Hartford County; area, 27
square miles .... Meriden.

Bristol; principal village of town of same name on Pequobuck
River; also on New York and New England R. R .... Meriden.

Broad; brook rising in northern part of North Stonington, flowing
northwest into Quinebaug River in northern part of Preston..... Moosup.

Broad; brook rising in eastern part of Ellington, flowing west into { Tolland.
Scantic River, in central part of East Windsor.   { Hartford.

Broad Brook; village in northeast part of Windsor................. Hartford.

Brockaway; island off western coast of Lyme in Connecticut River. Saybrook.

Bromica; mountain in eastern part of Kent; altitude, 1,380 feet .... New Milford.

Brookfield; town in northern part of Fairfield County; area, 21 { Danbury.
square miles.   { New Milford.

Brookfield; village in western part of town of same name on Still
River; also on Housatonic R. R..................................... Danbury.

Brookfield Center; village in central part of Brookfield............ Danbury.

Brookfield Junction; village in southern part of Brookfield on Housatonic R. R .... Danbury.

Brooklyn; town in central part of Windham County; area, 30 square { Woodstock.
miles.   { Putnam.

Brooklyn; principal village in central part of town of same name .. Putnam.

Brooks Vale; village in southwest part of Cheshire, on Northampton
division New York, New Haven and Hartford R. R............... New Haven.

Brown; point projecting from southern coast of Branford into Long
Island Sound .... New Haven.

Brown; brook, right branch of Mill River, in Fairfield............. Norwalk.

Buck; hill in northeastern part of Suffield; elevation, 260 feet ...... Springfield.

Names of sheets.

Buckland; village in northwest part of Manchester on New York and New England R. R... Hartford.

Buckwheat; hill in southern part of Meriden; elevation, 465 feet... Meriden.

Budington; pond in central part of Groton .... New London.

Bulkley; hill in southern part of Colchester; elevation, 520 feet..... Gilead.

Bull; mountain in southern part of Kent; altitude, 1,140 feet .... New Milford.

Bungee; brook in Woodstock, tributary to Still River, flowing into Black Pond.. Woodstock.

Bungee; hill in Woodstock; elevation, 870 feet .... Woodstock.

Bunker; hill in northwest part of Killingworth; elevation, 510 feet.. Guilford.

Bunnell; pond in northern part of Bridgeport .... Bridgeport.

Burlington; town in western part of Hartford County; area, 30 square miles.
{ Winsted.
Waterbury.
Granby.
Meriden.

Burlington; village in central part of town of same name........... Granby.

Burlington; brook rising in central part of Burlington, tributary to Farmington River.. Granby.

Burlington Station; village in western part of Avon, on Farmington River; also on New York, New Haven and Hartford R. R...... Granby.

Burnett Corner; village in northeast part of Groton................ Stonington.

Burnham; village in northern part of East Hartford, on New York and New England R. R., Springfield division .... Hartford.

Burnside; village in central part of East Hartford, on Hockanum River... Hartford.

Burnt; hill in eastern part of Farmington; elevation, 420 feet....... Meriden.

Burrville; village in northeast part of Torrington, on Still River; also, on New York, New Haven and Hartford R. R., Naugatuck division .... Winsted.

Burton; brook in western part of Salisbury, tributary to Salmon Creek .... Cornwall.

Bushnell; mountain in northwest part of Washington; altitude, 1,080 feet.. New Milford.

Bushy; point projecting from southwest coast of Groton into Long Island Sound .... New London.

Bushy; two hills in southern part of Granby; elevations, 500 and 480 feet, respectively... Granby.

Butternut; brook in western part of Litchfield tributary to Bantam River.. Waterbury.

Byram; river heading in New York, and flowing south through western part of Greenwich into Long Island Sound .... Stamford.

Byron; brook in northern part of Norwich, tributary to Shetucket River.. Norwich.

Calfpasture; island in Long Island Sound, forming part of Norwalk. Norwalk.

Calfpasture; point south of mouth of Norwalk River, in Norwalk .... Norwalk.

Calves; island off northwest coast of Old Lyme in Connecticut River. Saybrook.

Camp Meeting; village in western part of Windham .... Norwich.

Campville; village in southwest part of Harwinton on Naugatuck River, and on New York, New Haven and Hartford R. R......... Waterbury.

Canaan; town in northwest part of Litchfield County; area, 33 square miles.
{ Cornwall.
Winsted.
Sheffield.

Canaan; principal village in western part of North Canaan on Connecticut Western, and Housatonic R. Rs......................... Sheffield.

Bull. 117——2

Names of sheets.

Canaan; mountain in Canaan and North Canaan; highest summit being Mount Bradford, 1,927 feet ... { Cornwall. / Sheffield.

Canaan Valley; village in northeast part of North Canaan on Whiting River .... Sheffield.

Candlewood; range of mountains extending in western part of New Milford and eastern part of Sherman; greatest elevation, 1,000 feet .... New Milford.

Candlewood; hill in northwest part of Haddam; elevation, 480 feet. Guilford.

Candlewood Hill; brook in western part of Haddam, flowing northeast into Connecticut River in northern part of Haddam .... Guilford.

Cannon; village in Wilton on Norwalk River .... Norwalk.

Canterbury; town in southern part of Windham County; area, 40 square miles. ... { Woodstock. / Putnam. / Norwich. / Moosup.

Canterbury; village in east central part of town of same name on Quinebaug River .... Moosup.

Canton; town in western part of Hartford County; area, 30 square miles .... Granby.

Canton; village in southeast part of town of same name, on Central New England and Western R. R. .... Granby.

Canton Center; village in southwest part of town of same name.... Granby.

Carmel; mountain in northeast part of Hamden; altitude, 737 feet.. New Haven.

Carrington; hill in northeast part of Woodbridge; elevation, 420 feet. New Haven.

Cat Hole; mountain in northwest part of Meriden; altitude, 460 feet.. Meriden.

Cat Hole; brook in western part of Meriden, tributary to Sodom Brook... Meriden.

Cedar; mountain in Newington and Wethersfield; greatest altitude, 340 feet.. Middletown.

Cedar; point projecting into Long Island Sound from Westport..... Norwalk.

Cedar; pond in northeast part of Lyme............................ Saybrook.

Cedar; lake in central part of Chester........................... Saybrook.

Cedar; swamp in northeast part of Ledyard....................... Stonington.

Cedar; swamp in southeast part of North Stonington.............. Stonington.

Cedar; swamp in south central part of Chester................... Saybrook.

Cedar Swamp; brook in central part of Sterling, tributary to Moosup River .... Moosup.

Cedar Swamp; pond in southern part of Lebanon.................. Norwich.

Center Brook Station; village in east central part of Essex, on Connecticut Valley division, New York, New Haven and Hartford R. R. Saybrook.

Center Groton; village in north central part of Groton............ New London.

Centerville; village in east central part of Hamden............... New Haven.

Centerville Station; village in east central part of Hamden, on Northampton division New York, New Haven and Hartford R. R. New Haven.

Central; village in west central part of Plainfield, on Moosup River; also on Norwich and Worcester division New York and New England R. R.. Moosup.

Chaffeeville; village in Mansfield............................... Woodstock.

Chapinville; village in north central part of Salisbury........... Sheffield.

Chapinville Station; village in north central part of Salisbury, on Connecticut Western R. R....................................... Sheffield.

Chaplin; town in western part of Windham County; area, 20 square miles. ... { Norwich. / Woodstock.

Names of sheets.

Chaplin; village in town of same name............................. Woodstock.

Chaplin Station; village in southwest part of Hampton, and on New
York and New England R. R.. Woodstock.

Chapman; point projecting from southeast coast of Saybrook into
Long Island Sound.. Saybrook.

Chapman; hill in north central part of North Stonington; elevation,
520 feet... Stonington.

Chapman; pond in southwest part of East Haddam.................. Saybrook.

Charles; island off southern coast of Milford in Long Island Sound.. Bridgeport.

Chatham; town in northeast part of Middlesex County; area, 37 { Middletown.
square miles.   { Gilead.

Cherry; hill in western part of Branford; elevation, 166 feet........ New Haven.

Cherry; hill in southern part of Hamden; elevation, 220 feet......... New Haven.

Cherry; hill in eastern part of Middlefield; elevation, 300 feet...... Middletown.

Cherry; brook rising in southwest part of Granby, flowing southwest
through Canton into Farmington................................... Granby.

Cherry Brook; village in southwest part of Canton on Farmington
River and on Central New England and Western R. R........... Granby.

Cheshire; town in northern part of New Haven County; area, 38 { Meriden.
square miles.   { New Haven.

Cheshire; principal village in central part of town of same name... { Meriden.
                                                                   { New Haven.

Cheshire Street; village in eastern part of Cheshire on Meriden and
Waterbury R. R.. Meriden.

Chester; town in eastern part of Middlesex County; area, 11 square { Guilford.
miles.   { Saybrook.

Chester; principal village in eastern part of town of same name.... Saybrook.

Chesterfield; village in southwest part of Montville................. New London.

Chester Station; village in eastern part of Chester on Connecticut
River, also on Connecticut Valley division New York, New Haven
and Hartford R. R.. Saybrook.

Chestnut; hill in Wilton... Norwalk.

Chestnut; hill in northeast part of Killingly; elevation, 740 feet.... Putnam.

Chestnut; hill in western part of Chatham; elevation, 500 feet...... Middletown.

Chestnut; hill in northern part of Lebanon; elevation, 540 square
miles... Gilead.

Chestnut; hill in southern part of Killingworth; elevation, 348 feet. Guilford.

Chestnut; hill in eastern part of Oxford; elevation, 631 feet......... Derby.

Chestnut; hill in central part of Litchfield; elevation, 1,160 feet..... Waterbury.

Chestnut; mountain in southern part of Middletown; altitude, 620
feet... Middletown.

Chestnut Hill; village in eastern part of Killingly................... Putnam.

Chestnut Hill; village in eastern part of Columbia, on New York,
New Haven and Hartford R. R., Air Line division................ Gilead.

Chimon; island off mouth of Norwalk River in Long Island Sound.. Norwalk.

Choate; brook in Preston, tributary to Quinebaug River............ Norwich.

Church; hill in western part of North Canaan; elevation, 940 feet... Sheffield.

Clam; island off southwest coast of Branford, in Long Island Sound. New Haven.

Clapboard; hill in southeast part of Guilford; elevation, 108 feet... Guilford.

Clapboard; brook in northwest part of Bridgewater, tributary to
Housatonic River.. New Milford.

Clark; cove extending from Thames River into west coast of Ledyard. New London.

Clark Corner; village in southwest part of Hampton................ Woodstock.

Clark Falls; village in east central part of North Stonington, on Green
Fall River... Stonington.

Names of sheets.

Clayton; village in northern part of North Canaan on Konkapot River. Sheffield.

Clayville; village in northwest part of Griswold, on Norwich and
Worcester division New York and New England R. R............ Moosup.

Clayville; pond in northwest part of Griswold...................... Moosup.

Clear; brook in northern part of Burlington, tributary to Phelps
Brook ..../.............. Granby.

Clinton; town in southwest part of Middlesex County; area, 14 { Guilford.
square miles. { Saybrook.

Clinton; principal village in town of same name, also on Air Line
division, New York, New Haven and Hartford R. R.............. Guilford.

Clintonville; village in northeast part of North Haven .... New Haven.

Coatney; hill in Woodstock; elevation, 936 feet.................... Woodstock.

Cobalt; village in western part of Chatham, on Air Line division
New York, New Haven and Hartford R. R...................... Middletown.

Cobble; hill in western part of Kent; elevation, 940 feet............ New Milford.

Cockenoe; island in Long Island Sound, off mouth of Saugatuck
River .... Norwalk.

Coe; hill in northern part of Middlefield; elevation, 500 feet........ Middletown.

Coginchaug; river rising in northeast part of Guilford, flowing
through Middlefield and Middletown, into Sebethe River........ Guilford.

Colchester; town in northwest part of New London County; area, { Gilead.
50 square miles. { Norwich.

Colchester; borough in central part of town of same name, reached
by branch of New York, New Haven and Hartford R. R., Air Line
division .... Gilead.

Cold; brook in northern part of Norwich, tributary to Shetucket
River... Norwich.

Cold; brook in southern part of Glastonbury, tributary to Roaring
Brook .... Middletown.

Cold Spring; village in southeast part of Newtown, on Housatonic
R. R .... Danbury.

Colebrook; town in northeast part of Litchfield County; area, 34 { Sandisfield.
square miles. { Winsted.

Colebrook; village in central part of town of same name........... Winsted.

Colebrook River; village in northeast part of Colebrook, on Farmington River.. Sandisfield.

Colebrook Station; village in northwest part of Winchester, on Mad
River, also on Central New England and Western R. R.......... Winsted.

Collamer; village in extreme southern part of Sterling.............. Moosup.

Collins; hill in central part of Portland; elevation, 340 feet .... Middletown.

Collinsville; principal village in southwest corner of Canton on Farmington River, and also on New York, New Haven and Hartford R.
R.. Granby.

Columbia; town in southern part of Tolland County; area, 22 square { Gilead.
miles. { Norwich.

Columbia; village in central part of town of same name............ Gilead.

Compo; hill near coast in Westport .... Norwalk.

Compounce; pond in northwest part of Southington .... Meriden.

Congamuck; ponds forming boundary between Southwick, Mass., and
Suffield, Conn .... Granville.

Connecticut; river heading in Canada and northern New Hamp- { Springfield.
shire; forms boundary between New Hampshire and Vermont, { Hartford.
and flows southeast across Massachusetts and Connecticut into { Middletown.
Long Island Sound. { Guilford.
{ Saybrook.

Names of sheets.

Connecticut River; village in eastern part of Old Saybrook, on Connecticut River, also on Shore Line division New York, New Haven and Hartford R. R .... Saybrook.

Converse; hill in southern part of Stafford; elevation, 813 feet...... Tolland.

Cook; pond in southern part of Preston .... Stonington.

Copp; island off mouth of Norwalk River, in Long Island Sound.. Norwalk.

Copp; brook in Stonington.. Stonington.

Cornfield; point projecting from southern coast Old Saybrook into Long Island Sound.. Saybrook.

Cornwall; town in western part of Litchfield County; area, 47 square miles .... Cornwall.

Cornwall; village in town of same name............................ Cornwall.

Cornwall Bridge; village in southwest part of Cornwall, on Housatonic River, and on Housatonic R. R .... Cornwall.

Cornwall Center; village in central part of Cornwall............... Cornwall.

Cornwall Hollow; village in northeast part of Cornwall........... Cornwall.

Corum; hill in eastern part of Huntington; elevation, 400 feet...... Derby.

Coscob; village in southern part of Greenwich, on Coscob Harbor, and on New York, New Haven and Hartford R. R............... Stamford.

Coscob; harbor, arm of Long Island Sound indenting southern coast of Greenwich.. Stamford.

Cossaduck; hill in west central part of North Stonington; it has three peaks, the altitudes being 420, 420, and 460 feet, respectively. Stonington.

Cove; river in eastern part of Orange, flowing into Long Island Sound. New Haven.

Cove, The; pond in northeastern part of Wethersfield .... Middletown.

Coventry; town in southern part of Tolland County; area, 38 square { Tolland. miles. { Gilead.

Coventry; village in northwest part of town of same name.......... Tolland.

Cranberry; pond in southern part of Litchfield..................... Waterbury.

Cranberry; hill in western part of Madison; elevation, 400 feet..... Guilford.

Crane Bar; island off western coast of East Haven in New Haven Harbor .... New Haven.

Cream; hill in northern part of Cornwall; elevation, 1,503 feet...... Cornwall.

Cream Hill; pond in northern part of Cornwall..................... Cornwall.

Creek; pond in southern part of Sherman .... New Milford.

Crescent; beach on southeast coast of East Lyme, extending into Long Island Sound... New London.

Crescent; pond in northeast part of Southington.................... Meriden.

Cricker; brook, right-hand branch of Mill River, in Easton and Fairfield.. Norwalk.

Cromwell; town in northern part of Middlesex County; area, 13 square miles... Middletown.

Cromwell; principal village in southeast part of town of same name, on Connecticut River... Middletown.

Crow Hollow; brook rising in western part of Middletown, tributary to Harbor Brook... Meriden.

Crystal; pond on boundary line between Eastford and Woodstock.. Woodstock.

Danbury; town in northwest part of Fairfield County; area, 45 { Carmel. square miles. { Danbury.

Danbury; principal place in central part of town of same name, on Still River .... Danbury.

Danielsonville; borough in Brooklyn and Killingly, at junction of Five Mile River with Quinebaug River; also on Norwich and Worcester division New York and New England R. R................. Putnam.

Names of sheets.

Darien; town in southwest part of Fairfield County; area, 14 square $\{$ Stamford.
miles. $\}$ Norwalk.

Darien; village in town of same name .... Norwalk.

Darrow Rocks; islands off southwest coast of Branford, in Long
Island Sound.. New Haven.

Day; hill in central part of Windsor; elevation, 220 feet............. Hartford.

Daytonville; village in southern part of Torrington, on east branch of
Naugatuck River; also on New York, New Haven and Hartford R.
R., Naugatuck division... Winsted.

Dayville; village in northwest part of Killingly, on west bank Five
Mile River, opposite Killingly; also on Norwich and Worcester
division, New York and New England R. R...................... Putnam.

Deadman; brook; left branch of Saugatuck River, in Westport...... Norwalk.

Deep; brook, rises in western part of Newtown and flows northeast
into Pootatuck River.. Danbury.

Deep; river in southeast part of Colchester, tributary to Yantic River. Gilead.

Deep River; cove; arm of Connecticut River indenting coast between
Chester and Saybrook.. Saybrook.

Deep River; principal village in northeast part of Saybrook, on Connecticut River; also on Connecticut Valley division, New York,
New Haven and Hartford R. R .... Saybrook.

Deep River Station; village in northeast part of Saybrook, on Connecticut River; also on Connecticut Valley division, New York,
New Haven and Hartford R. R. .... Saybrook.

Derby; town in western part of New Haven County; area, 6 square
miles .... Derby.

Derby; village in southern part of town of same name, at junction of
Naugatuck and Housatonic rivers; also on Naugatuck division,
New York, New Haven and Hartford R. R. and New Haven and
Derby R. R... Derby.

Diamond; lake in eastern part of Glastonbury....................... Gilead.

Dickinson; creek rising in eastern part of Glastonbury, flowing south
through Marlboro into Salmon River, in Colchester.............. Gilead.

Dismal; brook in Southwick, Mass., and Granby.................... Granville.

Doaneville; village in east central part of Griswold and in Voluntown, on Pachaug River... Moosup.

Dodge; island off southwest coast of Stonington, in Long Island
Sound .... Stonington.

Dodge; pond in southeast part of East Lyme .... New London.

Dodgington; village in west part of Newtown .... Danbury.

Dog; pond in southern part of Goshen .... Winsted.

Dooley; pond in southwest part of Middletown .... Middletown.

Doolittle; pond in northeast part of Norfolk....................... Sandisfield.

Duck; river in western part of Old Lyme, tributary to Connecticut
River... Saybrook.

Durfy; hill in southwest part of Waterford; elevation, 120 feet...... New London.

Durham; town in western part of Middlesex County; area, 26 square
miles .... Guilford.

Durham; principal village in north central part of town of same
name.. Guilford.

Durham Center; village in central part of Durham .... Guilford.

Durham Meadows; swamp in central part of Durham, on both sides
Coginchaug River.. Guilford.

Dutton; mountain in central part of Norfolk; altitude, 1,620 feet.... Winsted.

Names of sheets.

Eagleville; village in western part of Marshfield, on Willimantic
River and on New London Northern R. R .... Tolland.

East; hill in northern part of Southbury; elevation, 660 feet......... Derby.

East; river rising in northeast part of Guilford, flowing south into
Guilford Harbor, Long Island Sound .... Guilford.

East Aspetuck; river rising in southern part of Warren, flowing
southwest through Washington into Housatonic, in central part of
New Milford.. New Milford.

East Berlin; village in southeast part of Berlin...................... Middletown.

East Branch; river in Ashford, tributary to Mount Hope River...... Woodstock.

East Branch; river rising in Salem, flowing southwest into Eightmile River, in northern part of Lyme............................ Saybrook.

East Branch Naugatuck; river rising in southeast part of Norfolk,
flowing south through Winchester into Naugatuck River, in extreme southern part of Torrington............................... Winsted.

East Branch Salmon; brook rising in northeast part of Hartland,
flowing southeast into Salmon Brook, in southeast part of Granby. Granville.

East Bridgeport; part of Bridgeport on Pequonnock River and on
New York, New Haven and Hartford R. R....................... Bridgeport.

East Bromica; hill in western part of Kent; elevation, 1,320 feet..... New Milford.

East Canaan; village in south central part of North Canaan, on Blackberry River; also on Connecticut Western R. R.................. Sheffield.

East Cornwall; village in southeast part of Cornwall .... Cornwall.

East Glastonbury; village in central part of Glastonbury .... Middletown.

East Granby; town in northern part of Hartford County; area, { Granby.
18 square miles.   { Hartford.

East Granby; village in town of same name .... Hartford.

East Great; plain in southern part of Norwich...................... Norwich.

East Haddam; town in eastern part of Middlesex County; area, 48 { Gilead.
square miles.   { Saybrook.

East Haddam; village in western part of town of same name, on Connecticut River .... Saybrook.

East Hampton; village in central part of Chatham................. Middletown.

East Hartford; town in eastern part of Hartford County; area, { Hartford.
18 square miles.   { Middletown.

East Hartford; principal village in northwest part of town of same
name, on New York and New England R. R., Springfield division. Hartford.

East Hartland; village in eastern part of Hartland .... Granby.

East Haven; town in southern part of New Haven County; area, 19
square miles .... New Haven.

East Haven; village in southeast part of town of same name, on Farm
River.. New Haven.

East Kent; village in east central part of Kent .... New Milford.

East Killingly; village in eastern part of Killingly, on Whitestone
Brook .... Putnam.

East; lake in northern part of Danbury............................ Danbury.

East Litchfield; village in eastern part of Litchfield, on Naugatuck
River; also on New York, New Haven and Hartford R. R., Naugatuck division .... Winsted.

East Lyme; town in southwest part of New London County; area, { Saybrook.
19 square miles.   { New London.

East Lyme; village in eastern part of town of same name, on Niantic
River.. New London.

East Meadow; brook rising in extreme southern part of Bethlehem,
flowing south into Nonewaug River, in central part of Woodbury. Waterbury.

Names of sheets.

East Meriden; village in eastern part of Meriden.................... Meriden.

East Morris; village in eastern part of Morris .... Waterbury.

East Mountain; range of mountains in southeastern part of Kent; greatest elevation being 1,320 feet.............................. New Milford.

East Norwalk; village in Norwalk, near mouth of Norwalk River and on New York, New Haven and Hartford R. R..................... Norwalk.

East Plymouth; village in northeast part of Plymouth............. Meriden.

East Port Chester; village in southwest part of Greenwich, on Byron River.. Stamford.

East Putnam; village in southern part of Putnam................... Putnam.

East River; village in southern part of Madison and station on Shore Line division New York, New Haven and Hartford R. R .... Guilford.

East Rock; hill in northeast part of New Haven; elevation, 359 feet. New Haven.

East Thompson; village in northeast part of Thompson, on New York and New England R. R.; also on Southbridge branch of same road. Webster.

East Village; village in northeast part of Monroe.................... Derby.

East Wallingford; village in southeast part of Wallingford, on Air Line division New York, New Haven and Hartford R. R........ New Haven.

East Willington; village in Willington.............................. Woodstock.

East Windsor; town in eastern part of Hartford County; area, 27 square miles.. Hartford.

East Windsor Hill; village in northwest part of South Windsor.... Hartford.

East Winsted; village directly east of Winsted on Still River, in eastern part of Winchester.. Winsted.

East Woodstock; village in northeast part of Woodstock, on Muddy Brook... Putnam.

Easter; hill in Pomfret; elevation, 720 feet........................... Woodstock.

Eastern; point projecting from southwest coast of Groton into Long Island Sound.. New London.

Eastford; town in western part of Windham County; area, 27 square miles... Woodstock.

Eastford; village in town of same name............................. Woodstock.

Easton; town in southern part of Fairfield County; area 29 square miles. ⎰ Danbury. / Norwalk. ⎱ Bridgeport.

Easton; village in central part of town of same name.............. ⎰ Norwalk. ⎱ Danbury.

Eightmile; brook rising in southeast part of Woodbury; flows south into Housatonic River, in southern part of Oxford................ Derby.

Eightmile; brook rising in southeast part of Woodbury; flowing south it forms boundary between Southbury, Middlebury, and Oxford, and empties into the Housatonic in southern part of Oxford. Waterbury.

Eightmile; river rising in extreme northwest corner of Southington, flowing in a southeasterly direction into Quinnipiac River, in southern part of Southington .... Meriden.

Eightmile; river rising in eastern part East Haddam, flowing southwest into Connecticut River in western part Lyme.............. Saybrook.

Eightmile River; cove, arm of Connecticut River indenting western coast of Lyme; is also the mouth of Eight Mile River........... Saybrook.

Elias; point projecting from southern coast of Greenwich into Greenwich Cove.. Stamford.

Elihus; island off southern coast of Stonington, in Little Narragansett Bay... Stonington.

Ellington; town in northwest part of Tolland County; area, 36 square miles. ⎰ Hartford. ⎱ Tolland.

Names of sheets.

Ellington; village in west central part of town of same name, on Springfield division New York and New England R. R............ Tolland.

Elliott; village in Pomfret .... Woodstock.

Ellithorpe; village in central part of Stafford .... Tolland.

Ellsworth; village in central part of Sharon......................... Cornwall.

Ellsworth; hill in southern part of Sharon; elevation, 1,580 feet.... Cornwall.

Elys Wharf; village in western part of Lyme, on Connecticut River. Saybrook.

Enfield; town in northeast part of Hartford County; area, 35 square {Springfield. miles. {Hartford.

Enfield; village in western part of town of same name.............. Hartford.

Essex; town in southeast part of Middlesex County; area, 13 square miles .... Saybrook.

Essex; principal village in east central part of town of same name, on Connecticut River; also, on Connecticut Valley division New York, New Haven and Hartford R. R............................... Saybrook.

Eureka Lake; pond in southern part of Danbury.................... Danbury.

Fairfield; town in southern part of Fairfield County; area, 51 square {Norwalk. miles. {Bridgeport.

Fairfield; village in town of same name............................. Norwalk.

Fairfield; beach off southern coast of Fairfield, facing Long Island Sound .... Bridgeport.

Fair Grounds; in western part of Danbury.......................... Danbury.

Fair Haven East; borough in eastern part of New Haven, just east of New Haven City, on the New York, New Haven and Hartford R. R .... New Haven.

Fair Oaks; village in central part of Montville..................... New London.

Fairy; lake in southeast part of Salem............................... New London.

Falls; village in western part of Canaan, on Housatonic River; also, on Housatonic R. R... Cornwall.

Falls; river rising in western part of Saybrook, flowing south into Westbrook, thence east through Essex into Connecticut River ... Saybrook.

Falls; mountain in southern part of New Milford .... New Milford.

Falls; brook rising in northwest part of Warren, flowing into the Housatonic in northeast part of Kent............................. Cornwall.

Falls; brook in southeast part of Wolcott, tributary to Tenmile River .... Meriden.

Falls River; cove, arm of Connecticut River indenting eastern coast of Essex .... Saybrook.

Farm; river rising in northwest part of Guilford, flowing southwest through North Branford, East Haven, into Long Island Sound... New Haven.

Farmill; river rising in southern part of Monroe, flowing southeast through Huntington into Housatonic River .... Derby.

Farmington; town in western part of Hartford County; area, 25 {Granby. square miles. {Meriden.

Farmington; village in central part of town of same name......... Meriden.

Farmington or **Tunxis**; river tributary to Connecticut River; is formed by two branches, east and west, which rise in Massachusetts and flow in a southeasterly direction through Colebrook, Hartland, and Barkhamsted, forming a single river in New Hartford, continuing south through Canton, forming boundary between Avon and Burlington, into Farmington, where it changes and flows in a northeastly direction through Avon and Simsbury, forming boundary between East Granby and Bloomfield, through Windsor, and flowing into the Connecticut River. {Granby. {Hartford. {Sandisfield.

Names of sheets.

Farmington, East Branch; river rising in southern part of Granville, Mass., flows south through Hartland and Barkhamsted into Farmington River in northeast part of New Hartford.................. Granville.

Farmington, West Branch; rises in Massachusetts, flows south and joins East Branch Farmington in northeastern part of New Hartford, and together they form the Farmington River.............. Winsted.

Fawn; brook rising in Hebron and flowing south into Blockledge River in southeast part of Marlboro .... Gilead.

Faxon; village in northeast part of East Haven .... New Haven.

Fayerweather; island off southwest coast of Bridgeport, in Long Island Sound .... Bridgeport.

Fenton; brook in Willington tributary to Fenton River............. Woodstock.

Fenwick; village in southeast part of Old Saybrook, on coast Long Island Sound; also, on Connecticut Valley division New York, New Haven and Hartford R. R .... Saybrook.

Fern; brook in northwest part of Watertown, tributary to branch of Naugatuck River .... Waterbury.

Ferry; point projecting from northeast coast of Old Saybrook into Connecticut River .... Saybrook.

Fish; island in Long Island Sound, off coast of Darien.............. Norwalk.

Fitchville; village in northern part of Bozrah, on Yantic River; also on New London Northern R. R .... Norwich.

Fivemile; point projecting from southwest of coast East Haven into Long Island Sound... New Haven.

Fivemile; river heading in northeast part of Thompson, flowing southwest through Thompson and Putnam into Quinebaug River in southwest part of Killingly .... Putnam.

Fivemile; brook in southern part of Oxford, tributary to Housatonic River .... Derby.

Fivemile; brook in southeast part of North Haven, flows west into Quinnipiac River in southern part of same town .... New Haven.

Fivemile; hill in central part of Oxford............................. Derby.

Fivemile; river in Fairfield County, flowing into Long Island Sound. Norwalk.

Fivemile River; station on New York, New Haven and Hartford R. R... Norwalk.

Flanders; village in east central part of East Lyme on Niantic River. New London.

Flanders; village in central part of Kent........................... New Milford.

Flat; hill in western part of Southbury; elevation, 698 feet......... Danbury.

Flirt; hill in western part of Easton; elevation, 535 feet............. Danbury.

Fluteville; village in southeast part of Litchfield, on Naugatuck River; also, on New York, New Haven and Hartford R. R ...... Waterbury.

Foot Rocks; group of islands off southern coast Branford, in Long Island Sound .... New Haven.

Forestville; village in southeast part of Bristol, on Pequabuck River; also, on New York and New England R. R........................ Meriden.

Forge; pond in northwest part of Salisbury......................... Sheffield.

Forge; brook in southern part of Sharon, tributary to Housatonic River.. Cornwall.

Fort; hill in central part of Groton; elevation, 220 feet.............. New London.

Fort Trumbull; village in east central part of New London, on Thames River.. New London.

Fourmile; river rising in northwest part of East Lyme, flowing south into Long Island Sound................................... Saybrook.

Names of sheets.

Fourmile; brook rising in southeast part of Oxford, flowing into Housatonic River, in western part of Seymour.................... Derby.

Fowlers; island off northeast coast of Stratford and west of Milford, in Housatonic River.. Bridgeport.

Franklin; town in northern part of New London County; area, 20 square miles... Norwich.

Franklin; village in central part of town of same name.............. Norwich.

Franklin Station; village in southwest part of Franklin, on Susquetonscut Brook; also on New London Northern R. R............. Norwich.

French; river heading in Massachusetts, flowing south into Connecticut, and joins the Quinebaug River, in southwest part of Thompson. $\left\{\begin{array}{l}\text{Webster.}\\\text{Putnam.}\end{array}\right.$

Freshwater; brook rising in northeast part of Enfield, flowing west through village of Thompsonville into Connecticut River........ Hartford.

Frog; pond in central part of Windham............................. Norwich.

Frog; brook in Windham, tributary to Shetucket River............. Norwich.

Frost; point projecting into Long Island Sound from Westport...... Norwalk.

Fuller; pond in northwest part of Kent............................ Cornwall.

Furnace; brook rising in northeast part of Stafford, tributary to Willimantic River... Tolland.

Gale Ferry; village in western part of Ledyard, on Thames River... New London.

Gardner; brook in Bozrah, tributary to Yantic River............... Norwich.

Gardner; hill in southwest part of New Milford; elevation, 540 feet. New Milford.

Gardner; lake lying on border between towns of Bozrah, Montville, and Salem.. Norwich.

Gaylordsville; village in northwest part of New Milford, on Housatonic River.. New Milford.

George; hill in southern part of Southbury; elevation, 560 feet...... Derby.

George Cellar; hill in western part of Orange; elevation, 230 feet... Derby.

Georgetown; village in northern part of Wilton, on Norwalk River; also on Danbury and Norwalk division of Housatonic R. R....... Danbury.

Giant; neck of land projecting from southern coast of East Lyme into Long Island Sound.. New London.

Gildersleeve; island west of town of Portland, in Connecticut River. Middletown.

Gilead; village in northern part of Hebron .... Gilead.

Glade; brook in eastern part of North Stonington, tributary to Green Fall River.. Stonington.

Glasko; village in southeast part of Griswold, on Pachaug River.... Moosup.

Glastonbury; town in southeastern part of Hartford County; area, 49 square miles. $\left\{\begin{array}{l}\text{Middletown.}\\\text{Gilead.}\end{array}\right.$

Glastonbury; village in northwest part of town of same name...... Middletown.

Glenville; village in southwest part of Greenwich, on Byram River.. Stamford.

Goat; brook rising in northwest part of Middlebury, tributary to Hop Brook .... Waterbury.

Goff; brook rising in southern part of Wethersfield, flows east into Connecticut, in eastern part of Rocky Hill .... Middletown.

Good; hill in southwestern part of Oxford; elevation, 593 feet....... Derby.

Good; hill in eastern part of Roxbury, extending in Woodbury; elevation, 1,005 feet... New Milford.

Goodspeed Landing; village in western part of East Haddam, on Connecticut River .... Saybrook.

Goose; island off northwest coast Old Lyme, in Connecticut River .. Saybrook.

Goose; island off east coast New London, in Thames River .... New London.

Goose; hill in southwest part of Haddam; elevation, 620 feet....... Guilford.

Names of sheets.

Goshen; town in central part of Litchfield County; area, 44 square miles. — Cornwall. / Winsted.

Goshen; village in south central part of town of same name........ Winsted.

Goshen; village in southern part of Lebanon .... Norwich.

Goshen; point projecting from southern coast of Waterford into Long Island Sound...... New London.

Governor; one of the Thimble Islands lying off southern coast of Branford, in Long Island Sound ...... New Haven.

Granby; town in northwest part of Hartford County; area, 42 square miles. — Granville. / Granby.

Granby; village in eastern part of town of same name ...... Granby.

Granby Station; village in southwestern part of East Granby, on Central New England and Western R. R ...... Granby.

Graniteville; village in southern part of Waterford...... New London.

Grassy; island near the Norwalk Islands off mouth of Norwalk River and Long Island Sound...... Norwalk.

Grassy; hill in eastern part of Lyme; elevation, 368 feet...... Saybrook.

Grassy; hill in northwest part of Orange, having two summits, altitude of each being 270 feet...... Derby.

Grassy Plain; village in the western part of Bethel, on Umpog Creek. Danbury.

Gravelly; brook in eastern part of Woodstock, tributary to Muddy Brook ...... Putnam.

Great; brook in eastern part of New Milford, tributary to Housatonic River...... New Milford.

Great; brook, left-hand branch of Sasco Brook, in Fairfield .... Norwalk.

Great; brook rising in western part of Montville, flowing south into Niantic River...... New London.

Great; brook in Groton, tributary to Poquonoc River...... New London.

Great; brook in northern part of Farmington, tributary to the Farmington River...... Meriden.

Great; hill in southwest part of Seymour; elevation, 640 feet........ Derby.

Great; hill in northeast part of Naugatuck; elevation, 540 feet...... Waterbury.

Great; hill in southeast part of Woodbury; elevation, 930 feet...... Waterbury.

Great; hill in Portland and Chatham; elevation, 700 feet ...... Middletown.

Great; island off southwest coast of Old Lyme, in Connecticut River, separated from Old Lyme by Back River...... Saybrook.

Great; mountain in southeast part of Sherman; elevation, 1,040 feet New Milford.

Great; pond in northeast part of Ridgefield ...... Danbury.

Great Bare; mountain in eastern part of New Milford; altitude, 1,075 feet ...... New Milford.

Great Hill; pond in southeast part of Portland ...... Middletown.

Great Meadow; brook in northern part of Voluntown, tributary to Pachaug River ...... Moosup.

Green; harbor off eastern coast of New London, in Thames River.... New London.

Green; island off southern coast of Branford, in Long Island Sound.. New Haven.

Green; mountain in southwest part of New Milford, lying partly in Sherman; altitude, 1,100 feet ...... New Milford.

Green; pond in southeast part of Sherman ...... New Milford.

Green Fall; river heading in southeast part of Voluntown, flowing south through North Stonington into Pawcatuck River, in western part of Hopkinton, R. I ...... Moosup.

Greenfarm; village in Westport...... Norwalk.

Greenfield Hill; village in Fairfield...... Norwalk.

Greenville; village in western part of Preston, on Quinebaug River. Norwich.

GANNETT.] A GEOGRAPHIC DICTIONARY OF CONNECTICUT. **29**

Names of sheets.

Greenwich; town in souhwest part of Fairfield County; area, 49
square miles.. Stamford.

Greenwich; borough in southern part of town of same name, on Long
Island Sound, and also on New York, New Haven and Hartford
R. R.. Stamford.

Greenwich; creek rising in eastern part of town of same name, flowing south into Indian Harbor...................................... Stamford.

Greenwich; cove, arm of Long Island Sound indenting southeastern
coast of Greenwich .... Stamford.

Greenwich; point projecting from southeastern coast of Greenwich
into Long Island Sound.. Stamford.

Greer; hill in northwestern part of Ledyard; elevation, 340 feet..... New London.

Greer; hill in northwestern part of Griswold; elevation, 360 feet.... Moosup.

Greystone; village in southwestern part of Plymouth, on Hancock
Brook, also on New York and New England R. R................. Waterbury.

Gridley; mountain in northwestern part of Salisbury; altitude, 2,200
feet... Sheffield.

Gridley; pond in eastern part of Harwinton........................ Waterbury

Griswold; town in northeastern part of New London County; area,
37 square miles... Moosup.

Griswold; point projecting from southwestern coast of Old Lyme
into Long Island Sound.. Saybrook.

Griswold; island off southern coast East Lyme in Long Island Sound. New London.

Griswoldville; village in southern part of Wethersfield............ Middletown.

Grosvenordale; village in west central part of Thompson, on French
River, also on Norwich and Worcester division, New York and
New England R. R......,.. Putnam.

Groton; town in southern part of New London County; area, 35 { New London.
square miles.   { Stonington.

Groton; principal village in east central part of town of same name,
on Thames River, reached by New York, Providence and Boston
R. R... New London.

Groton Long; point projecting from southeastern coast of Groton
into Long Island Sound.. New London.

Grove; beach off southern coast Clinton and Westbrook, on Long
Island Sound.. Saybrook.

Grove Beach; village in southeastern part of Clinton, on Shore Line
division, New York, New Haven and Hartford R. R.............. Saybrook.

Guardhouse; point projecting from southeastern coast Old Saybrook
into Long Island Sound.. Saybrook.

Guernsey; hill in southeastern part of Litchfield; elevation, 860 feet. Waterbury.

Guilford; town in southeastern part of New Haven County; area, 50
square miles.. Guilford.

Guilford; borough in southern part of town of same name, on West
River, reached by Shore Line division, New York, New Haven and
Hartford R. R... Guilford.

Guilford; harbor extending into coast of town of same name, off
Long Island Sound.. Guilford.

Guilford; point on southern coast of town of same name, projecting
into Long Island Sound.. Guilford.

Guilford Station; village in southern part of Guilford, on Shore Line
division, New York, New Haven and Hartford R. R .... Guilford.

Gull Rocks; islands off southwest coast of Branford, in Long Island
Sound .... New Haven.

Gully; brook rising in southeastern corner of Bloomfield, tributary to
Park River .... Hartford.

Names of sheets.

Gumman; hill on boundary between Wilton and Norwalk; elevation, 280 feet.. Norwalk.

Gungywamp; hill in southwestern part of Ledyard; elevation, 340 feet .... New London.

Gurleyville; village in Marshfield.................................... Woodstock.

Haddam; town in central part of Middlesex County; area, 46 square miles. ⎰ Middletown. ⎱ Gilead. ⎰ Guilford. ⎱ Saybrook.

Haddam; village in northern part of town of same name on Connecticut Valley division, New York, New Haven and Hartford R. R... Guilford.

Haddam; island in Connecticut River, in northeast part of town of same name.. Guilford.

Haddam Neck; strip of land forming northeast coast of Haddam, lying east of Connecticut River and west of Salmon River........ Saybrook.

Hadlyme; village in East Haddam and Lyme......................... Saybrook.

Hadlyme Landing; village in northwest corner Lyme, on Connecticut River... Saybrook.

Hadlyme Station; village in northeast part of Chester, on Connecticut River and on Connecticut Valley division, New York, New Haven and Hartford R. R .... Saybrook.

Halfway; river rising in southern part of Newtown, flowing northeast into Housatonic River, forming part of boundary between Newtown and Monroe... Derby.

Hall; hill in northwest part of Somers; elevation, 320 feet .... Palmer.

Hall Meadow; brook rising in southern part of Norfolk, flowing through northeast part of Goshen into Naugatuck River, in northwest part of Torrington... Winsted.

Hallenbeck; river rising in eastern part of Cornwall, flowing north, then west into Housatonic River, in western part of Canaan...... Cornwall.

Hamburg; village in west central part of Lyme, on Eightmile River. Saybrook.

Hamden; town in southern part of New Haven County; area, 34 square miles... New Haven.

Hammertown; village in north central part of Salisbury........... Sheffield.

Hammonasset; beach off southeast coast of Madison, projecting into Long Island Sound... Guilford.

Hammonasset; river rising in southeast part of Durham, flowing south, forming boundary between Killingworth, Clinton, and Madison, into Long Island Sound.................................... Guilford.

Hammonasset; point projecting from Hammonasset beach into Long Island Sound .... Guilford.

Hampton; town in western part of Windham County; area, 26 square miles. ⎰ Woodstock. ⎱ Norwich.

Hampton; village in central part of town of same name............. Woodstock.

Hampton Station; village in northwest part of Hampton, and on New York and New England R. R .... Woodstock.

Hancock; village in southern part of Plymouth, on Hancock Brook, also on New York and New England R. R......................... Waterbury.

Hancock; brook rising in southwestern part of Bristol, flows through southern Plymouth into Naugatuck River, in northern part of Waterbury.. Waterbury.

Hanging; several hills in southwestern part of Berlin and northwestern Meriden; West Peak, elevation, 1,007 feet; South Mountain, 790 feet, and peak with no name, 877 feet..................... Meriden.

Names of sheets.

Hank; hill in Mansfield... Woodstock.

Hanover; village in northern part of Sprague, on Little River...... Norwich.

Hanover; brook in northern part of Newtown, tributary to Housatonic River... Danbury.

Hannover; pond in southwestern part of Meriden................... Meriden.

Harbor; brook rising in eastern part of Meriden, tributary to Quinnipiac River. It has three branches: North and South and Cro Hollow Brook.. Meriden.

Harrisville; village in extreme southeastern corner of Woodstock, on Muddy Brook.. Putnam.

Hart; brook rising in northern part of Goshen, flowing into Naugatuck River, in northwestern part of Torrington................... Winsted.

Hartford; city and town coextensive, situated in Hartford County, on Connecticut River, is reached by New York, New Haven and Hartford, New York and New England, Central New England and Western, Hartford and Connecticut Valley railroads; **area 17** square miles. } Middletown. Hartford.

Hartland; town in northwestern part of Hartford County; area, 34 square miles. { Sandisfield. Winsted. Granville. Granby.

Harts; ponds in western part of Berlin.............................. Meriden.

Harwinton; town in eastern part of Litchfield County; area, 34 square miles. { Winsted. Granby.

Harwinton; village in north central part of town of same name.... Winsted.

Hatch; pond in southwest part of Kent .... New Milford.

Hatchet; pond in northwestern part of Woodstock .... Brookfield.

Hatchet; hill in northwestern part of Woodstock, extending into Southbridge, and having four peaks, elevations being 1,040, 1,020, and 1,020 feet, respectively..................................... Brookfield.

Hatchett; point projecting from southeastern coast Old Lyme into Long Island Sound... Saybrook.

Hattertown; village in southern part of Newtown................... Danbury.

Hawleyville; village in northwestern part of Newtown on Pond River; is reached by Housatonic R. R., by New York and New England R. R., and by Shepang, Litchfield and Northern R. R........ Danbury.

Hatcock; point projecting from southern coast Branford into Long Island Sound .... New Haven.

Hayden; village in northeastern part of Windsor, on Hartford division of New York, New Haven and Hartford R. R............... Hartford.

Haystack; mountain in northwestern part of Norfolk; altitude, 1,680 feet.. Sandisfield

Hazardville; village in central part of Enfield..................... Hartford.

Head; harbor extending into southern coast of Guilford .... Guilford.

Hearthstone; hill in southeastern part of Franklin; elevation, 540 feet.. Norwich.

Hebron; town in southern part of Tolland County; area, 37 square miles .... Gilead.

Hebron; village in eastern part of town of same name.............. Gilead.

Hedgehog; hill in Stafford; elevation, 1,100 feet................... Woodstock.

Higby; mountain in western part of Middletown and in Middlefield; altitude, 920 feet.. Middletown.

Higganum; village in northern part of Haddam, on Candlewood Hill Brook .... Guilford.

Names of sheets.

High; one of the Thimble Islands, lying off southern coast of Branford, in Long Island Sound... New Haven.

High; hill in central part of Madison; elevation, 396 feet.............. Guilford.

High Ridge; village in extreme northern part of Stamford........... Stamford.

High Rock Grove; village in northern part of Beacon Falls, on Naugatuck River.. Derby.

Highland; village in western part of Middletown, on Meriden, Waterbury and Connecticut River R. R................................... Middleton.

Highland; lake in southeastern part of Winchester................... Winsted.

Hinckley; hill in eastern part of Stonington; elevation, 200 feet..... Stonington.

Hoadley; point projecting from southwestern coast of Guilford into Long Island Sound .... Guilford.

Hockanum; river rising in Shenipsit Lake, flows into the Connecticut River.   { Hartford.   Tolland.

Hockanum, South Branch; branch of Hockanum River, rising in southeastern part of Manchester, and flows into main river in western part of town... Hartford.

Hockanum; brook rising in Bethany, flows west into Naugatuck River in central part of Beacon Falls............................. Derby.

Hog; northern branch of Park River, rises in northern part of Bloomfield and flows south through that town, then through northeastern part of West Hartford, and joins the south fork Park River in west central part of Hartford....................................... Hartford.

Hog; pond in southeastern part of Lyme............................. Saybrook.

Hogshead; point on southwestern coast of Madison, projecting into Long Island Sound... Guilford.

Holly; tidal pond, on coast of Darien............................... Norwalk.

Holt; hill in northwestern part of Plymouth; elevation, 960 feet..... Waterbury.

Honey Pot; brook rising in central part of Cheshire, flows northeast into Quinnipiac River, in northeast part of same town........... Meriden.

Hooe Tower; hill in southwestern Bloomfield and extending into Simsbury; elevation, 960 feet.................................... Granby.

Hop; river tributary to Willimantic River, rises in southwestern part of Tolland, flows south through Vernon, Bolton, Coventry, and Andover, forming a boundary between Coventry and Columbia.   { Tolland.   Gilead.

Hop; brook in northern part of Brookfield tributary to Housatonic River.. Danbury.

Hop; brook rising in northeastern part of Canton, flows east into Farmington River in east central part of Simsbury .... Granby.

Hop; brook rising in northwestern part of Middlebury, flows southeast into Naugatuck River in northern part of Naugatuck........ Waterbury.

Hop Swamp; hill in eastern part of Middlebury; elevation, 600 feet. Waterbury.

Hopeville; village in northwestern part of Griswold, on Pachaug River.. Moosup.

Hopeville; village in southern part of Waterbury, on Naugatuck River; also, on Naugatuck division New York, New Haven and Hartford R. R.. Waterbury.

Hopkins; hill in eastern part of Naugatuck; elevation, 830 feet...... Derby.

Hopp; brook rising in western part of Bethany, tributary to Bladen River.. Derby.

Horse; one of the Thimble islands, lying off southern coast of Branford, in Long Island Sound... New Haven.

Horse; hill in western part of Westbrook; elevation, 100 feet....... Saybrook.

Horseneck; point projecting from southwestern coast of Greenwich into Long Island Sound... Stamford.

Names of sheets.

Horseneck; brook rising in northeastern part of Greenwich, flows south into Long Island Sound .... Stamford.

Horton; cove extending from Thames River into southeastern coast of Montville .... New London.

Horton; point projecting from southwestern part of Branford into Long Island Sound .... New Haven.

Hotchkissville; village in central part of Woodbury, on Pomperaug River .... Waterbury.

Housatonic; river rising in Berkshire County, Mass., flows southward into Connecticut, intersecting Litchfield County, and forms the boundary between Fairfield and New Haven, and enters Long Island Sound in Bridgeport.
{ Cornwall.
Clove.
Danbury.
Bridgeport.
Derby.
Sheffield.

Hubbell; hill in eastern part of Sherman; elevation, 940 feet .... New Milford.

Hull; hill in western part of Oxford; elevation, 420 feet .... Derby.

Hungry; hill in southern part of Guilford; elevation, 214 feet .... Guilford.

Huntington; town in eastern part of Fairfield County; area, 31 square miles .... Derby.

Huntington; village in central part of town of same name .... Derby.

Huntington; hill in western part of Naugatuck; elevation, 850 feet. Derby.

Huntingtown; village in southern part of Newtown .... Danbury.

Huntsville; village in south central part of Canaan on Hallenbeck River .... Cornwall.

Hut; hill in eastern part of Bridgewater; elevation, 860 feet .... New Milford.

Iasco; brook flowing into Long Island Sound, along boundary between Fairfield and Westport .... Norwalk.

Indian; harbor, arm of Long Island Sound, indenting southern coast of Greenwich .... Stamford.

Indian; pond in extreme corner of Sharon, on boundary between New York and Connecticut .... Cornwall.

Indian; mountain in northwestern part of Sharon and southwestern part of Salisbury, greatest elevation being 1,420 feet .... Cornwall.

Indian; river rises in Orange, flows south through Milford into Long Island Sound .... Bridgeport.

Indian Head; hill in northeastern part of New Haven; elevation, 320 feet .... New Haven.

Indian Neck; narrow strip projecting from southern part of Branford into Long Island Sound .... New Haven.

Iron; hill in northeastern part of New Milford; elevation, 1,040 feet. New Milford.

Island; brook in western part of Bridgeport, tributary to Pequonnock River .... Bridgeport.

Ivorton; village in western part of Essex........................... Saybrook.

Ivy; mountain in northern part of Goshen; altitude, 1,640 feet...... Winsted.

Jack; brook rising in northeastern part of Roxbury, flows south, thence west into Shepaug River in southwest part of Roxbury.. New Milford.

Jack; brook in northern part of Oxford, tributary to Little River... Derby.

Jefferson; hill in eastern part of Litchfield; elevation, 1,220 feet.... Waterbury.

Jeremy; brook in southeastern part of Southbury, tributary to Eight Mile Brook .... Derby.

Jerusalem; village in southwestern part of New Milford, on Rocky River.. New Milford.

Jewett; village in northwestern part of Griswold, on Quinebaug River, also on Norwich and Worcester division New York and New England R. R .... Moosup.

Bull. 117——3

Names of sheets.

Jewett; village in central part of Lisbon, on New York and New England R. R., Providence division .... Norwich.

Job; pond in southern part of Portland .... Middletown.

John Johnson; hill in central part of Southbury; elevation, 400 feet. Derby.

Johnson; point projecting from southwest coast of Branford in Long Island Sound .... New Haven.

Jones; hill in southern part of Orange; elevation, 120 feet .... New Haven.

Jordan; village in southern part of Waterford .... New London.

Jordan; creek in southwestern part of Waterford, flowing into Long Island Sound .... New London.

Jordan; brook rising in north central part of Waterford; flows south into Jordan Creek .... New London.

Joshua; point projecting from southern coast of Guilford into Long Island Sound .... Guilford.

Joshua; cove extending into town of Guilford .... Guilford.

Joyceville; village in northern part of Salisbury .... Sheffield.

Judd; brook in northern part of Colchester, tributary to Salmon River Gilead.

Judd Bridge; village in northwestern part of Roxbury, on Shepaug River; also on Shepaug, Litchfield and Northern R. R .... New Milford.

Kanosha; lake in western part of Danbury .... { Danbury. { Carmel.

Keeny Cove; pond in northwest part of Glastonbury; extends into southern part of East Hartford .... Middletown.

Kelsey; point projecting from southern coast of Old Saybrook into Long Island Sound .... Saybrook.

Kensington; village in northern part of Berlin .... Meriden.

Kent; town in western part of Litchfield County; area, 48 square miles. { Clove. { Cornwall. { New Milford.

Kent; principal village in west central part of town of same name, on Housatonic R. R .... New Milford.

Kent; range of mountains in central part of town of same name, greatest elevation being 1,340 feet .... New Milford.

Kenyonville; village in Woodstock .... Woodstock.

Ketch; brook rising in western part of Ellington; flows west into Scantic River, in southern part of East Windsor .... Hartford.

Kettle; creek, right-hand branch of Saugatuck River, in Weston .... Norwalk.

Kettletown; brook rising in central part of Southbury; flows into Housatonic River, in central part of same town .... Derby.

Keyser; island at mouth of Norwalk River, in Norwalk .... Norwalk.

Killingly; town in eastern part of Windham County; area, 50 square miles .... Putnam.

Killingly; village in northwest part of town of same name, on east bank of Fivemile River, and also on Norwich and Worcester division New York and New England R. R .... Putnam.

Killingly Center; village in central part of Killingly, on Whetstone Brook .... Putnam.

Killingworth; town in southwestern part of Middlesex County; area, 36 square miles .... Guilford.

Killingworth; village in central part of town of same name .... Guilford.

Kimball; hill in northeastern part of Hampton; elevation, 745 feet.. Woodstock.

King; island lying off southwest coast of East Haven, in New Haven Harbor .... New Haven.

King; island lying in Connecticut River between southern part of towns of Suffield and Enfield .... Hartford.

Names of sheets.

Kirby; brook in southern part of Washington, tributary to Shepaug River .... New Milford.

Kitemaug; village in southeastern part of Montville, on Thames River; also on New London and Northern R. R.................... New London.

Knowlton; brook in Ashford, tributary to Mount Hope River....... Woodstock.

Knowlton; hill in southwest corner of Ashford; elevation, 600 feet.. Woodstock.

Kohanza; pond in northwestern part of Danbury .... Danbury.

Konomoc; hill in northwestern part of Waterford; elevation, 389 feet .... New London.

Lake Pond; brook in northwestern part of Waterford, tributary to Niantic River .... New London.

Lakeville; village in south central part of Salisbury................. Cornwall.

Lamentation; range of mountains extending through east part of Berlin and Meriden, the two highest peaks having an altitude of 725 and 654 feet, respectively...................................... Meriden.

Lanesville; village in southwestern part of New Milford, on Still River.. New Milford.

Lantern; hill in western part of North Stonington; elevation, 520 feet.. Stonington.

Lantern Hill; pond in east central part of Ledyard, on boundary between that town and North Stonington .... Stonington.

Latimer; hill in northern part of Thomaston; elevation, 1,022 feet .. Waterbury.

Laurel; hill in extreme southeastern part of Norwich; elevation, 340 feet .... Norwich.

Laurel Glen; village in eastern part of North Stonington, on Green Fall River .... Stonington.

Laysville; village in northwestern part of Old Lyme................. Saybrook.

Lead Mine; brook rising in southeastern part of Torrington; flows south through Harwinton into Naugatuck River in northeastern part of Thomaston. } Waterbury. Winsted.

Lead Mine; hill in Union; elevation, 1,240 feet..................... Woodstock.

Lebanon; town in northwestern part of New London County; area, 56 square miles. } Gilead. Norwich.

Lebanon; village in northern part of town of same name............ Norwich.

Lebanon Station; village in eastern part of Lebanon, on New London Northern R. R .... Norwich.

Lebanon Street; village in central part of Lebanon .... Norwich.

Ledyard; town in central part of New London County; area, 41 square miles. } New London. Stonington.

Ledyard; village in central part of town of same name .... New London.

Leesville; village in northwestern part of East Haddam, on Salmon River.. Gilead.

Leete; island off southwestern coast of Guilford in Long Island Sound. Guilford.

Leete Island; village in southwestern part of Guilford, on Shore Line division New York, New Haven and Hartford R. R .... Guilford.

Leonard; pond in southwestern part of Kent .... New Milford.

Leonard Bridge; village in western part of Lebanon, on New York, New Haven and Hartford R. R., Air Line division............... Gilead.

Lewis; island off southeastern coast of Branford, in Long Island Sound .... New Haven.

Lewis; gut, arm of Long Island Sound indenting southwest coast of Stratford .... Bridgeport.

Liberty; hill in northern part of Lebanon; elevation, 500 feet........ Gilead.

5 GRAPC DICIONARY OF CONNECTICUT. [BULL. 117.

Names of sheets.

Lieutenant; river rises in southern part of Lyme, flows southwest into Connecticut River, in west central part of Old Lyme......... Saybrook.

Lime Rock; village in southeastern part of Salisbury............... Cornwall.

Lindley; brook in eastern part of Wolcott, tributary to Mad River .. Meriden.

Linsley; pond in southern part of North Branford................... New Haven.

Lion Head; hill in northwestern part of Salisbury; elevation, 1,760 feet .... Sheffield.

Lisbon; town in northern part of New London County; area, 16 square miles. { Norwich. / Moosup.

Litchfield; town in central part of Litchfield County; area, 57 square miles. { Cornwall. / New Milford. / Winsted. / Waterbury.

Litchfield, borough in central part of town of same name .... { Waterbury. / Winsted.

Little; river rising in northern part of Hampton; flows south into Shetucket River, in southeastern part of Sprague. { Woodstock. / Norwich.

Little; river rising in northern part of Oxford; flows southeast into Naugatuck River, in northwest part of Seymour................... Derby.

Little; harbor in southwestern coast of Guilford .... Guilford.

Little; pond in northeastern part of Ridgefield .... Danbury.

Little; pond in central part of Litchfield............................. Waterbury.

Little; pond in northeastern part of Thompson........................ Webster.

Little; pond in central part of Winchester............................ Winsted.

Little City; village in western part of Haddam .... Guilford.

Little Mount Tom; mountain in northeastern part of Washington; altitude, 1,100 feet... New Milford.

Little Narragansett; bay, arm of Long Island Sound, indenting southeastern coast of Stonington and southwestern coast of Rhode Island.. Stonington.

Lockwood; pond in northern part of Watertown .... Waterbury.

Long; beach off southern coast of Stratford extending into Long Island Sound .... Bridgeport.

Long; brook in western part of Brookfield, tributary to Still River.. Danbury.

Long; brook in northeastern part of Brooklyn, tributary to Quinebaug River.. Putnam.

Long; cove, extending from Thames River into southwestern coast of Ledyard.. New London.

Long; hill in western part of Middletown; elevation, 260 feet........ Middletown.

Long; hill in southeastern part of Haddam, having two peaks, altitude of each being 520 feet .... Guilford.

Long; hill in western part of Guilford; elevation, 300 feet........... Guilford.

Long; hill in southeastern part of Huntington; elevation, 381 feet... Derby.

Long; hill in southwestern part of North Stonington................. Stonington.

Long; island off eastern coast of Stratford in Housatonic River...... Bridgeport.

Long; pond in northeastern part of Thompson....................... Webster.

Long; pond on boundary between Ledyard and North Stonington.... Stonington.

Long; range of mountains in northwestern part of New Milford, greatest elevation being 1,080 feet .... New Milford.

Long Hill; village in northern part of Trumbull on Pequonnock River, also on Housatonic R. R................................... Derby.

Long Ledge; island off southern coast of East Lyme, in Long Island Sound.. New London.

Names of sheets.

Long Meadow; brook rising in northwestern part of Middlebury, flows southeast into Naugatuck River in central part of Naugatuck.. Waterbury.

Long Meadow; pond in southern part of Middlebury.............. { Waterbury. Derby.

Long Meadow; pond in northern part of Bethlehem, extending into Morris .... Waterbury.

Long Meadow Pond; brook rising in western part of Naugatuck, tributary to Naugatuck River...................................... Derby.

Long Neck; point projecting into Long Island Sound from Darien.. Norwalk.

Long Ridge; village in northern part of Stamford................... Stamford.

Long Society; village in western part of Preston.................... Norwich.

Long Swamp; brook in eastern part of Middlebury, tributary to Hop Brook.. Waterbury.

Lord; bay extending from Connecticut River into west coast Old Lyme and Lyme.. Saybrook.

Lord; cove, a continuation of Lord Bay, extending into southwestern coast of Lyme.. Saybrook.

Lord; hill in southwestern part of Lyme; elevation, 279 feet........ Saybrook.

Lord; island off southwestern coast of East Haddam, in Connecticut River.. Saybrook.

Lower White; hill in northern part of Huntington; elevation, 600 feet.. Derby.

Lyman Viaduct; village in western part of Colchester on Salmon River; also on New York, New Haven and Hartford R. R........ Gilead.

Lyme; town in southwestern part of New London County; area, 37 square miles.. Saybrook.

Lyme; principal village in Old Lyme, in west central part of town. Saybrook.

Lyme Station; village in west central part of Old Lyme, on Connecticut River, and also on shore line division New York, New Haven and Hartford R. R.. Saybrook.

Lyon Plain; village in Weston.................................... Norwalk.

Macedonia; village in western part of Kent, on Macedonia Brook .. New Milford.

Macedonia; brook rising in southwestern part of Sharon, flows south { New Milford. into Houstonic River in Kent. Cornwall.

Mad; river rising in northern part of Wolcott, flows southwest through that town into Naugatuck River, in central part of Waterbury... Meriden.

Mad; river rising in central part of Norfolk, flows southeast into Still River, in east central part of Winchester........................... Winsted.

Madison; town in southeastern part of New Haven County; area, 39 square miles.. Guilford.

Madison; village in southern part of town of same name, and on Shore Line division New York, New Haven and Hartford R. R.... Guilford.

Maltby; three lakes in northeastern part of Orange.................. New Haven.

Mamacoke; village in northwestern part of Groton, on Thames River.. New London.

Mamacoke; hill in extreme eastern part of Waterford, on point projecting into Thames River... New London.

Mamanaseo; pond in west central part of Ridgefield.............. Carmel.

Manchester; town in eastern part of Hartford County; area, 21 square miles. { Hartford. Middletown. Tolland. Gilead.

Names of sheets.

Manchester; village in north centra. part of town of same name, on Hockanum River.. Hartford.

Manchester Green; village in central part of Manchester .... Hartford.

Manetock; hill in western part of Waterford; elevation, 240 feet.... New London.

Mansfield; town in eastern part of Tolland County; area, 47 square miles. { Tolland. Woodstock. Gilead. Norwich.

Mansfield; village in northwestern part of town of same name...... Tolland.

Mansfield Center; village in Mansfield............................... Woodstock.

Mansfield Depot; village in northwestern part of Mansfield on Willimantic River .... Tolland.

Mansfield Hollow; village in Mansfield............................. Woodstock.

Marbledale; village in northwestern part of Washington on Aspetuck River... New Milford.

Margerie; pond in extreme northern part of Danbury................ Danbury.

Marion; village in southwestern part of Southington................ Meriden.

Marlboro; town in southeastern part of Hartford County; area, 24 square miles. { Middletown. Gilead.

Marlboro; village in central part of town of same name............. Gilead.

Marlboro; pond in western part of town of same name.............. Gilead.

Maromas; village in northeastern part of Middletown on Connecticut River... Middletown.

Marsh; brook, tributary to Poland River, rising in Marsh Pond in extreme northeast corner of Plymouth............................. Meriden.

Marsh; pond in northwest corner of Bristol.......................... Meriden.

Marsh; hill in central part of Orange; elevation, 200 feet........... New Haven.

Mashamoquet; brook rising in western part of Pomfret, flows east into Quinebaug River, in southeastern part of same town........ Putnam.

Mashapaug; village in northern part of Union on Mashapaug Pond.. Brookfield.

Mashapaug; pond in northern part of Union......................... Brookfield.

Mashentuck; hill in central part of Killingly; elevation, 560 feet... Putnam.

Mason; island off southwest coast of Stonington, in Long Island Sound and east of Mystic Harbor................................. Stonington.

Mason; point projecting from southern coast of Mason Island into Long Island Sound .... Stonington.

Massapeag; village in east central part of Montville on Thames River. New London.

Maynard; hill in western part of Ledyard; elevation, 180 feet...... New London.

McCook; point projecting from southeast coast of East Lyme into Long Island Sound .... New London.

Meadow; brook rising in southern part of Windsor, flows south into Connecticut River, in northeast part of Hartford .... Hartford.

Mean; brook rising in northeastern part of Monroe, flows southeast into Farmill River, in central part of Huntington................ Derby.

Mechanicsville; village in southwestern part of Thompson, on Quinebaug River .... Putnam.

Meeting-House; brook rising in southern part of Meriden, flows south into Quinnipiac River, in northern part of Wallingford.......... Meriden.

Melrose; village in northeastern part of East Windsor, on Springfield division of New York and New England R. R..................... Hartford.

Menunketesuck; point projecting from southern coast of Westbrook into Long Island Sound.. Saybrook.

Menunketesuck; river in southern part of Westbrook, flows into Long Island Sound... Saybrook.

Names of sheets.

Meriden; town in northeastern part of New Haven County; area, 23 square miles. — Meriden. New Haven. Middletown. Guilford.

Meriden; city and principal place in town of same name, on New York, New Haven and Hartford R. R., and on Meriden and Waterbury R. R .... Meriden.

Merrick; brook rising in southern part of Hampton, flows through Scotland into Shetucket River.................................... Norwich.

Merritt; hill in northern part of Stonington; elevation, 260 feet..... Stonington.

Merrow; village in northwestern part of Mansfield, on New London Northern R. R., also on Willimantic River......................... Tolland.

Merwin; brook in central part of Brookfield, tributary to Hop Brook. Danbury.

Merwinsville; village in northwestern part of New Milford, on Housatonic R. R... New Milford

Meshapock; brook in southern part of Middlebury, tributary to Hop Brook .... Waterbury.

Meshhomasick; mountain in northeastern part of Portland, extending into Chatham; greatest elevation, 860 feet.................... Middletown.

Mianus; village in southeastern part of Greenwich, on Mianus River. Stamford.

Mianus; river heading in New York, flows south through Stamford into Greenwich; thence into Coscob Harbor...................... Stamford.

Middle; river rising in northern part of Stafford; tributary to the Willimantic River .... Tolland.

Middle Haddam; village in western part of Chatham, on Connecticut River .... Middletown.

Middlebury; town in northwestern part of New Haven County; area, 19 square miles. — Waterbury Derby.

Middlebury; village in central part of town of same name.......... Waterbury.

Middlefield; town in northwestern part of Middlesex County; area, 15 square miles. — Middletown. Guilford.

Middlefield; village in southern part of town of same name, on New York, New Haven and Hartford R. R .... Middletown.

Middlefield Center; village in central part of Middlefield, on New York, New Haven and Hartford R. R........................... Middletown.

Middletown; town in northern part of Middlesex County; area, 44 square miles. — Middleton. Guilford.

Middletown; principal place in northern part of town of same name, on Connecticut River .... Middletown.

Miles; mountain in northeastern part of Salisbury; altitude, 1,140 feet .... Sheffield.

Milford; town in southwestern part of New Haven County; area, 23 square miles. — Bridgeport. Derby. New Haven.

Milford; principal village of town of same name; situated in south central part, on Wepawaug River................................. Bridgeport.

Milford; point projecting from southwestern coast of Milford into Long Island Sound.. Bridgeport.

Mill; brook rising in central part of Plainfield, flows west into Quinebaug River in southeastern part of Canterbury .... Moosup.

Mill; brook rising in western part of Sharon and flows into New York. Cornwall.

Mill; cove extending from Thames River into southwestern coast of Ledyard.. New London.

Mill; creek in southern part of Old Lyme, flows into Long Island Sound. Saybrook.

Names of sheets.

Mill; creek in northeastern part of Haddam; tributary to Connecticut River.. Gulford.

Mill; hill in central part of Colchester; elevation, 480 feet........... Gilead.

Mill; river heading in Poundbridge, N. Y., flows south through Stamford into Stamford Cove... Stamford.

Mill; river rising in Cheshire, flows through Hamden into New Haven Harbor.. New Haven.

Mill; river rising in western part of Monroe, flows south, forming boundary between Monroe, Trumbull, and Easton; thence through Fairfield into Long Island Sound. } Norwalk. Danbury.

Mill Brook; village in southwestern part of Colebrook............. Winsted.

Mill Plain; village in Fairfield..................................... Norwalk.

Mill Plain; village in western part of Danbury on New York and New England R. R... Carmel.

Mill Rock; hill in southeastern part of Hamden; elevation, 200 feet. New Haven.

Milldale; village in southern part of Southington on Tenmile River. Meriden.

Miller; pond in northeastern part of Waterford .... New London.

Millington; village in east central part of East Haddam .... Saybrook.

Millstone; point projecting from southwest corner of Waterford into Long Island Sound.. New London.

Millville; village in western part of Naugatuck on Long Meadow Pond Brook .... Derby.

Milton; village in northwestern part of Litchfield.................. Cornwall.

Mine; hill in southeastern part of New Milford; elevation, 860 feet. New Milford.

Minnehaush; mountain in northeastern part of Glastonbury; highest elevation, 720 feet.. Middletown.

Minortown; village in eastern part of Woodbury .... Waterbury.

Misery; brook in southeastern part of Southington, tributary to Quinnipiac River .... Meriden.

Mixville; village in western part of Cheshire .... Meriden.

Mohawk; brook in western part of Barkhamsted, flows into west branch of Farmington River in southern part of town.......... Winsted.

Mohawk; pond in southeastern part of Cornwall................... Cornwall.

Mohawk; mountain in southeastern part of Cornwall; greatest elevation, 1,600 feet... Cornwall.

Mohegan; village in northeastern part of Montville on Thames River. New London.

Mohegan; hill in eastern part of Montville; elevation, 340 feet...... New London.

Monroe; town in eastern part of Fairfield County; area, 27 square miles. } Danbury. Derby.

Monroe; village in eastern part of town of same name .... Derby.

Montowese; village in southern part of North Haven on New York, New Haven and Hartford R. R .... New Haven.

Montville; town in central part of New London County; area, 46 square miles. } Norwich. New London.

Montville; village in southeastern part of town of same name on Oxoboro Brook .... New London.

Montville; village in southeastern part of town of same name on Thames River.. New London.

Montville; hill in central part of Montville; elevation, 400 feet...... New London.

Moodus; village in northwestern part of East Haddam .... } Saybrook. Gilead.

Moody Mill; pond in southwestern part of Fairfield, on boundary line...... .... Bridgeport.

Moore; brook in central part of Salisbury, tributary to Salmon Creek } Cornwall. Sheffield.

Names of sheets.

Moose; hill in southeastern part of Oxford; elevation, 670 feet....... Derby.

Moose; hill in southwestern part of Guilford; elevation, 260 feet .... Guilford.

Moosehorn; brook in northern part of Roxbury, tributary to Shepaug River...... New Milford.

Moosehorn; hill in northern part of Roxbury; elevation, 1,020 feet.. New Milford.

Moose Meadow; village in Willington............ Woodstock.

Moosup; pond in northeastern part of Plainfield.............. Moosup.

Moosup; river rising in western part of Rhode Island, flows west
through Sterling and Plainfield into Quinebaug River in northwestern part of Plainfield.......... Moosup.

Moosup; village in central part of Plainfield, on Moosup River...... Moosup.

Morgan; point projecting from southwestern part of East Haven
into Long Island Sound......... New Haven.

Morgan; pond in southern part of Ledyard............ New London.

Morris; town in central part of Litchfield County; area, 19 square { New Milford.
miles.   { Waterbury.

Morris; village in central part of town of same name............. Waterbury.

Morris; cove extending into southwestern coast of East Haven from
Long Island Sound....... New Haven.

Morris Station; village in western part of Morris on Shepaug River. New Milford.

Mountain; brook in northeastern part of Danbury, tributary to
Wood Creek....... Danbury.

Mountain; brook in northwestern part of Cheshire, tributary to Tenmile River....... Meriden.

Mount Carmel; village in northern part of Hamden, on Northampton
division, New York, New Haven and Hartford R. R............. New Haven.

Mount Hope; river rising in extreme southern part of Union, flows
through Ashford and joins the Fenton in southeast corner of Mansfield, where they flow into the Natchaug River.................. Woodstock.

Mount Hope; village in Mansfield....... Woodstock.

Mount Misery; brook rising in southeastern corner of Plainfield,
flows south into Pachaug River in west central part of Voluntown. Moosup.

Mount Misery; hill on boundary between Griswold and Voluntown;
elevation, 420 feet .... Moosup.

Mount Tom; pond in southwestern part of Litchfield, in Morris and
Washington .... New Milford.

Mud; brook in northern part of Seymour, tributary to Naugatuck
River....... Derby.

Mud; brook flowing into Long Island Sound, in Westport.......... Norwalk.

Mud; pond in western part of Norfolk......... Winsted.

Muddy; brook rising in Agawam, Mass., flows south into Stony brook
in southeastern part of Suffield....... Hartford.

Muddy; brook rising in Southbridge, Mass., flows southeast through
Woodstock into Quinebaug River, in northwestern part of Putnam Putnam.

Muddy; pond in northern part of Woodstock .... Brookfield.

Mudge; pond in northwestern part of Sharon .... Cornwall.

Mulberry; point on southern coast of Guilford, projecting into Long
Island Sound .... Guilford.

Mulberry; hill in eastern part of Naugatuck; elevation, 700 feet..... Derby.

Mullen; hill in western part of Canterbury; elevation, 585 feet...... Norwich.

Mumford; cove extending from Long Island Sound into southern
coast of Groton....... New London.

Mystic; harbor, arm of Long Island Sound indenting southern coast
of New London County, between Groton and Stonington .... Stonington.

Names of sheets.

Mystic; island off southwestern coast of Stonington, in Long Island Sound.. Stonington.

Mystic; river heading in Ledyard and North Stonington, flows south, forming boundary between North Stonington, Stonington, and Groton and Ledyard, thence into Mystic Harbor. } New London. Stonington.

Mystic; village in western part of Stonington on Mystic River...... Stonington.

Mystic Bridge; village in southwestern part of Stonington, on Mystic River.. Stonington.

Mystic River; village in eastern part of Groton, on Mystic River.... Stonington.

Natchaug; river rising in central part of Woodstock, flows south through Ashford and Chaplin into Shetucket River in northeastern part of Windham... Woodstock.

Naugatuck; town in northwestern part of New Haven County; area, 17 square miles. { Waterbury. Derby.

Naugatuck; village in town of same name on Naugatuck River...... Derby.

Naugatuck; river rising in Norfolk, runs southward through New Haven County into Housatonic River. { Winsted. Waterbury. Derby.

Naugatuck Junction; village in southwestern part of Milford, on the Housatonic River... Bridgeport.

Nells; island off southwest corner of Milford in Housatonic River... Bridgeport.

Nepaug; village in west central part of New Hartford, on Nepaug River.. Winsted.

Nepaug; river rises in eastern part of Torrington, flows southeast through New Hartford into Farmington River, in southwest part of Canton. } Granby. Winsted.

Neversink; pond on southern boundary between New Fairfield and Danbury.. Danbury.

New Boston; village in northwestern part of Thompson, on Quinebaug River.. Webster.

New Britain; town in southern part of Hartford county; area, 14 square miles.. Meriden.

New Britain; city in town of same name in south central part of the town on New York and New England R. R....................... Meriden.

New Canaan; town in southwestern part of Fairfield County; area, 23 square miles. { Stamford. Norwalk.

New Canaan; borough in town of same name .... Norwalk.

New Fairfield; town in northern part of Fairfield County; area, 11 square miles. { Clove. New Milford. Carmel. Danbury.

New Fairfield; village in southern part of town of same name...... Danbury.

New Hartford; town in eastern part of Litchfield County; area, 38 square miles. { Winsted. Granby.

New Hartford; principal village in town of same name, located in northeastern part, on west branch of Farmington River .... Granby.

New Haven; town in southern part of New Haven County; area, 13 square miles.. New Haven.

New Haven; city in town of same name, and county seat of New Haven County.. New Haven.

New Haven; harbor, arm of Long Island Sound, indenting southern coast of New Haven County, between Orange, New Haven, and East Haven.. New Haven.

Names of sheets.

New London; city in southern part of New London County; area, 6 square miles .... New London.

New Milford; town in southwestern part of Litchfield County; area, 63 square miles. { Clove. } New Milford. { Danbury.

New Milford; principal village in town of same name, situated a little to the south of central part of the town, on Housatonic River. New Milford.

New Preston; village in northwestern part of Washington, on Aspetuck River .... New Milford.

New Preston Station; village in central part of Washington, on Shepaug River .... New Milford.

Newent; village in central part of Lisbon .... Norwich.

Newfield; village in northern part of Torrington, on east branch of Naugatuck River .... Winsted.

Newfield; village in extreme northern part of Middletown, on Middletown branch New York, New Haven and Hartford R. R....... Middletown.

Newington; town in southern part of Hartford County; area, 14 { Meriden. square miles. { Middletown.

Newington; village in eastern part of town of same name........... Middletown.

Newington Junction; village in northern part of Newington, on New York and New England R. R. and New York, New Haven and Hartford R. R .... Middletown.

Newtown; town in northern part of Fairfield County; area, 60 { Danbury. square miles. { Derby.

Newtown; borough in central part of town of same name .... Danbury.

Niantic; principal village in East Lyme, in southeastern part of town, at the mouth of Niantic River .... New London.

Niantic; river formed by two tributaries, Great Brook and Lakes Pond Brook; forms partial boundary between Waterford and East Lyme, and flows into Long Island Sound......................... New London.

Nichol; pond in south central part of Oxford....................... Derby.

Nichol Farms; village in southeastern part of Trumbull............ Bridgeport.

Nickerson; hill in central part of Lyme; elevation, 485 feet .... Saybrook.

Nineveh Falls; village in western part of Killingworth............. Guilford.

Noank; village in southeastern part of Groton, on Mystic Harbor ... Stonington.

Nonewaug; river rising in northeastern part of Bethlehem, flows southwest through that town into Pomperaug River, in central part of Woodbury .... Waterbury.

Norfolk; town in northern part of Litchfield County; area, 17 square { Sandisfield. miles. { Cornwall. { Winsted.

Norfolk; principal village in town of Norfolk, in central part of town, on Central New England and Western R. R..................... Winsted.

North; cove, arm of Connecticut River, indenting southeast coast of Old Saybrook... Saybrook.

North; pond in western part of Lebanon, on boundary line between Hebron and Lebanon .... Gilead.

North Ashford; village in Eastford .... Woodstock.

North Bloomfield; village in extreme northeastern part of Bloomfield .... Hartford.

North Branch; river rising in south part of Burlington, tributary to Pequabuck River .... Meriden.

North Branch; river in eastern part of Meriden, tributary to Harbor Brook .... Meriden.

Names of sheets.

North Branch; river in northeastern part of Granby, tributary to
Salmon Brook .... Granby.

North Branford; town in southern part of New Haven County; { New Haven.
area, 27 square miles.   { Guilford.

North Branford; village in southern part of town of same name, on
Branford Harbor.. New Haven.

North Bridgeport; village, part of Bridgeport City, on Pequonnock
River... Bridgeport.

North Canaan; town in northwestern part of Litchfield County;
area, 19 square miles.

⎧ Litchfield.
⎨ Sandisfield.
⎩ Cornwall.
  Winsted.

North Canton; village in northern part of Canton .... Granby.

North Colebrook; village in northwestern part of Colebrook, on
Sandy Brook .... Sandisfield.

North Cromwell; village in eastern part of Cromwell, on Valley division New York, New Haven and Hartford R. R .... Middletown.

North Franklin; village in northwestern part of Franklin.......... Norwich.

North Granby; village in northern part of Granby .... Granby.

North Grosvenor Dale; village in west central part of Thompson, on
French River .... Putnam.

North Guilford; village in northwestern part of Guilford........... Guilford.

North Haven; town in southern part of New Haven County; area, 21
square miles .... New Haven.

North Haven; village in central part of town of same name, on Quinnipiac River .... New Haven.

North Kent; village in northeastern part of Kent, on Housatonic
River.. Cornwall.

North Lyme; village in central part of Lyme, on Beaver Brook...... Saybrook.

North Madison; village in central part of Madison .... Guilford.

North Plains; village in southeastern part of East Haddam......... Saybrook.

North Somers; village in northern part of Somers.................. Palmer.

North Spectacle; pond in eastern part of Kent..................... New Milford.

North Stamford; village in northeastern part of Stamford .... Stamford.

North Stonington; town in eastern part of New London County; { Moosup.
area, 57 square miles.   { Stonington.

North Stonington; village in southern part of town of same name,
on Shunock River.. Stonington.

North Wilton; village in Wilton.................................... Norwalk.

North Woodstock; village in northeastern part of Woodstock ..... Putnam.

Northfield; village in southeastern part of Litchfield .... Waterbury.

Northfield; hill in southeastern part of Litchfield; elevation, 1,150
feet .... Waterbury.

Northford; village in northwestern part of North Branford .... New Haven.

Northford Station; village in eastern part of North Haven, on New
York, New Haven and Hartford R. R.................................... New Haven.

Northville; village in northeastern part of New Milford, on East
Aspetuck River.. New Milford.

Norton; village in Darien.. Norwalk.

Norton; south point of Belle Island, in Norwalk.................... Norwalk.

Norton; river rising in New Canaan; flows south, forming boundary
between Darien and Stamford, into Long Island Sound .... Stamford.

Norwalk; town in southwestern part of Fairfield County; area, 25
square miles.. Norwalk.

Names of sheets.

Norwalk; borough in town of same name, near mouth of Norwalk
River, on New York, New Haven and Hartford R. R............. Norwalk.

Norwalk; group of islands off mouth of Norwalk River, forming
part of Norwalk... Norwalk.

Norwalk; river rising in northeastern part of Ridgefield; flows south { Norwalk.
through Wilton and Norwalk into Long Island Sound.   { Danbury.

Norwich; town in north central part of New London County; area, { Norwich.
28 square miles.   { New London

Norwich; city in town of Norwich, on Thames River .... Norwich.

Norwich Town; village in western part of Norwich, on Yantic
River... Norwich.

Norwich; pond in southeastern part of Lyme........................ Saybrook.

Nott; island off southeastern part of Lyme, in Connecticut River.... Saybrook.

Noyes; river rising in eastern part of West Hartford; flows south into
South Fork Park River, in southeastern corner of West Hartford. Hartford.

Nut Plains; village in southeastern part of Guilford................. Guilford.

Oakville; village in extreme northwestern part of Waterbury, on
Steel Brook and on New York, New Haven and Hartford R. R.,
Watertown branch.. Waterbury.

Obwebetuck; hill in southwestern part of Windham; elevation, 661
feet... Norwich.

Occum, village in northeastern part of Norwich on Shetucket River. Norwich.

Ocean; beach extending from southern coast of New London into
Long Island Sound.. New London.

Old Lyme; town in southwestern part of New London County; area,
27 square miles .... Saybrook.

Old Saybrook; town in southeastern part of Middlesex County;
area, 18 square miles... Saybrook.

Old Saybrook; principal village in town of same name, situated in
east central part of town on Shore Line division and also on Connecticut Valley division New York, New Haven and Hartford R. R. Saybrook.

Oneco; village in east central part of Sterling, on New York and New
England R. R., Providence division............................. Moosup.

Orange; town in southwestern part of New Haven County; area, 31 { Bridgeport.
square miles.   { Derby.
                                                                { New Haven.

Orange Center; village in Orange.................................... Derby.

Orcuttville; village in central part of Stafford, on Middle River and
also on the New London Northern R. R.......................... Tolland.

Ore Hill; village in western part of Salisbury on Central New England and Western R. R... Cornwall.

Osborne; village in central part of East Windsor, on Springfield division New York and New England R. R .... Hartford.

Osprey; beach on southern coast of New London and on Long Island
Sound .... New London.

Oswegatchie; hill in southeastern part of East Lyme; elevation, 240
feet .... New London.

Ox; hill in central part of Norwich; elevation, 380 feet .... Norwich.

Oxford; town in western part of New Haven County; area, 33 square
miles .... Derby.

Oxford; village in town of same name in central part on Little River. Derby.

Oxoboro; brook, rises in northwestern part of Montville, flows southeast into Thames River in southeast part of same town.......... New London.

Oxoboro; lake in northwestern part of Montville.................... New London.

Oyster; river in eastern part of Orange; flows into Long Island Sound. New Haven.

Names of sheets.

Oyster; river, rises in northern part Old Saybrook; flows into Long Island Sound .... Saybrook.

Oyster; point projecting from southern part of New Haven Harbor.. New Haven.

Oyster; point projecting from southern part of Orange into Long Island Sound .... New Haven.

Pachaug; pond in south central part of Griswold.................... Moosup.

Pachaug; river heading in Western Rhode Island, flows west through Voluntown and Griswold into Quinebaug River in northwestern part of Griswold.. Moosup.

Pachaug; village in central part of Griswold, on Pachaug River.... Moosup.

Packersville; village on boundary between Canterbury and Plainfield, situated on Mill Brook .... Moosup.

Paine; hill in Pomfret; elevation, 705 feet........................... Woodstock.

Painters Ridge; mountain in northern part of Roxbury, extending into Washington; altitude, 1,100 feet........................... New Milford.

Park; pond in southwestern part of Winchester.................... Winsted.

Park; river in Hartford, tributary to Connecticut River............. Hartford.

Park Lane; village in central part of New Milford.................. New Milford.

Parnassus; mountain in central part of East Haddam; altitude, 615 feet .... Saybrook.

Parrish; hill in Scotland, Windham, and Chaplin; elevation, 620 feet. Norwich.

Pataguanset; lake in central part of East Lyme .... New London.

Pataguanset; river rising in central part of East Lyme; flows south into Long Island Sound... New London.

Patchogue; river, rises in central part of Westbrook; flows south into Long Island Sound .... Saybrook.

Patton; brook in northeastern part of Southington tributary to Quinnipiac River .... Meriden.

Pautipaug; hill in western part of Sprague; elevation, 400 feet...... Norwich.

Pawcatuck; river heading in Rhode Island; flows west forming eastern boundary of Stonington and partial boundary of North Stonington, thence into Little Narragansett Bay................. Stonington.

Peak; mountain in northeastern part of East Granby; altitude, 665 feet.. Hartford.

Pecausett; pond in southwestern part of Portland.................. Middletown.

Peck; hill in northwestern part of Woodbridge; elevation, 500 feet.. Derby.

Peet; hill in northern part of New Milford; elevation, 1,193 feet.... New Milford.

Pemberwick; village in southwestern part of Greenwich........... Stamford.

Pembroke; pond on boundary between Bridgeport and Stratford... Bridgeport.

Pendleton Hill; village in northeasten part of North Stonington.... Moosup.

Penny; island off southeastern coast of Groton in Mystic Harbor and on New York, Providence and Boston R. R...................... Stonington.

Pequabuck; river rising in northern part of Plymouth, flows southeast through Bristol into Plainville where it takes a northerly course into Farmington River in central part of Farmington. } Waterbury. Meriden.

Pequonnock; river flowing through Trumbull and Bridgeport into Long Island Sound. { Derby. Bridgeport.

Pequot; hill in eastern part of Groton; elevation, 180 feet.......... Stonington.

Perkins; mountain in northeastern part of Somers, having two peaks, altitude of peaks being 980 and 840 feet, respectively............ Palmer.

Phelps; brook in northern part of Burlington, tributary to Farmington River.. Granby.

Phelps; brook in western part of North Stonington, tributary to Shunock River... Stonington.

Phœnixville; village in Eastford .... Woodstock.

Names of sheets.

Pickerel; lake in southwestern part of Colchester, extending into
East Haddam.. Gilead.
Pine; brook in northern part of North Haven, tributary to Quinnipiac
River.. New Haven.
Pine; brook in western part of Bethany tributary, to Bladen River.. Derby.
Pine; brook rising in northwestern part of Chatham, flows southeast
into Salmon River, in northwestern part of East Haddam........ Middletown.
Pine; brook in western part of Colchester, tributary to Salmon
River.. Gilead.
Pine; hill in western part of Plymouth; elevation, 980 feet. .... Waterbury.
Pine; island off southwestern coast of Groton, in Long Island Sound. New London.
Pine; mountain in central part of Norfolk; altitude, 1,520 feet..... Winsted.
Plne; point projecting into Long Island Sound from Norwalk....... Norwalk.
Pine; river rising in southern part of Wallingford, flows south into
Five Mile Brook, in southeastern part of North Haven............ New Haven.
Pine Bridge; village in southern part of Beacon Falls, on Naugatuck
River.. Derby.
Pine Creek; point projecting into Long Island Sound from Fair-
field... Norwalk.
Pine Meadow; village in northeastern part of New Hartford, on
west branch of Farmington River .... Granby.
Pine Orchard; village in southern part of Branford, on Shore Line
division New York, New Haven and Hartford R. R .... New Haven.
Pine Rock; hill in Hamden and New Haven; altitude, 271 feet ..... New Haven.
Pinnacle; hill in northern part of Washington; elevation, 1,280 feet. New Milford.
Pisgah; mountain in south central part of Durham, having two peaks,
altitude of each being 640 feet. .... Guilford.
Pisgah; hill in western part of Oxford, extending into Southbury;
elevation, 620 feet .... Derby.
Pisgah; mountain in central part of Colebrook; altitude, 1,440 feet.. Sandisfield.
Pistapaug; mountain in southwestern part of Durham, greatest eleva-
tion being 640 feet .... Guilford.
Pistapaug; pond in Durham, Wallingford, North Branford, and
Guilford.. Guilford.
Plain; hill in northwestern part of Norwich; elevation, 480 feet..... Norwich.
Plainfield; town in southern part of Windham County; area, 44 ⎰ Putnam.
square miles.   ⎱ Moosup.
Plainfield; village in south central part of Plainfield, at junction of
two branches of New York and New England R. R .... Moosup.
Plainfield Junction; village in western part of Plainfield, at junction
of two branches of New York and New England R. R........... Moosup.
Plainville; town in southwestern part of Hartford County; area, 9
square miles .... Meriden.
Plainville; principal village in town of same name on Pequabuck
River .... Meriden.
Plane; brook rising in northwestern part of Westbrook, tributary to
Menunketesuck River.. Saybrook.
Plantsville; village in southern part of Southington, on Quinnipiac
River, and also on New York, New Haven and Hartford R. R .... Meriden.
Pleasant; beach on southwestern coast of Waterford, extending into
Long Island Sound .... New London.
Pleasant Valley; village in southern part of Barkhamsted.......... Granby.
Pleasure; hill in northern part of Franklin; elevation, 520 feet...... Norwich.
Plumb; hill in central part of Litchfield; elevation, 960 feet .... Waterbury.
Plumb; hill in southern part of Washington; elevation, 1,070 feet... New Milford.

Names of sheets.

Plymouth; town in southeastern part of Litchfield County; area, 22 ⎰ Waterbury.
square miles.   ⎱ Meriden.

Plymouth; principal village in town of same name, located in western part of the town .... Waterbury.

Pocotopaug; creek in Chatham, tributary to Pine Brook .... Middletown.

Pocotopaug; lake in northeastern part of Chatham .... Middletown.

Podunk; river rising in northeastern part of South Windsor, flows into Connecticut River, in northwest corner of East Hartford .... Hartford.

Poland; river rising in eastern part of Harwinton, flows south into Pequabuck River .... Waterbury.

Polkville; village in northeastern part of Bristol .... Meriden.

Polls; hill in southeastern part of Montville; elevation, 520 feet ..... New London.

Pomfret; town in central part of Windham County; area, 42 square ⎰ Woodstock.
miles.   ⎱ Putnam.

Pomfret; village in northeastern part of town of same name .... Putnam.

Pomfret Center; village in northeastern part of Pomfret .... Putnam.

Pomfret Landing; village in southeastern part of Pomfret, on Mashamoquet Brook .... Putnam.

Pomfret Station; village in central part of Pomfret, on New York and New England R. R. .... Putnam.

Pomfret Street; village in northeastern part of Pomfret .... Putnam.

Pomperaug; river rising in northeastern part of Bethlehem, flows ⎛ Derby.
south through Woodbury into Housatonic River, in southern ⎨ Danbury.
part of Southbury.   ⎝ Waterbury.

Pomperaug; village in southern part of Woodbury, on Pomperaug River .... Waterbury.

Pomperaug Valley; village in central part of Southbury .... Derby.

Pond; brook rising in southern part of Brookfield, flows northeast through northwest part of Newtown into Housatonic River .... Danbury.

Pond; hill in southeastern part of Wallingford; elevation, 340 feet .. New Haven.

Pond; hill in northern part of Cornwall; elevation, 1,425 feet .... Cornwall.

Pond; mountain in northern part of New Fairfield; altitude, 1,120 feet .... New Milford.

Pond; point projecting from southeast coast of Milford into Long Island Sound .... Bridgeport.

Pond Meadow; village in northern part of Westbrook, on Falls River .... Saybrook.

Pond Meadow; swamp in southwestern corner of Haddam, extending into Killingworth .... Guilford.

Pond Rock; range of mountains extending along eastern part of East Haven into Branford and North Branford .... New Haven.

Ponset; village in central part of Haddam .... Guilford.

Poquetanock; village in southwestern part of Preston .... New London.

Poquetanock; cove extending from Thames River into western coast Ledyard and Preston .... New London.

Poquonoc; lake in central part of Groton .... New London.

Poquonoc; plain in southwestern part of Groton on Long Island Sound .... New London.

Poquonoc; river in southwestern part of Groton; flows south into Long Island Sound .... New London.

Poquonoc; village in northern part of Windsor on Farmington River .... Hartford.

Poquonoc Bridge; village in southwestern part of Groton .... New London.

Pootatuck; river rising in southern part of Newtown; flows north into Housatonic River, in northern part of the town .... Danbury.

Names of sheets.

Popes Flat; island between Stratford and Milford, in Housatonic River.. Bridgeport.

Poplar Swamp; brook rising in central part of Avon; flowing into Farmington River in northern part of Farmington .... Meriden.

Portland; town in northern part of Middlesex County; area, 26 square miles.. Middletown.

Portland; principal village in town of same name; on New York, New Haven and Hartford R. R. and Connecticut River .... Middletown.

Post; light-house off eastern coast of Saybrook in Connecticut River .... Saybrook.

Pot; one of the Thimble Islands, lying off southern coast of Branford, in Long Island Sound.. New Haven.

Potter; pond in Woodstock... Woodstock.

Powder; island off east coast of New London in Thames River ...... New London.

Powder; brook in eastern part of Harwinton, tributary to Poland River .... Winsted.

Power; lake in central part of East Lyme........................... New London.

Pratt; cove, arm of Connecticut River, indenting eastern coast of Saybrook .... Saybrook.

Prentice; mountain in northwestern part of North Stonington; altitude, 540 feet.. Stonington.

Preston; town in north central part of New London County; area, 33 square miles.
{ Norwich. Moosup. New London. Stonington. }

Preston; principal village in town of same name, situated in east central part of town... Moosup.

Preston; village in western part of town of same name on Quinebaug River.. Norwich.

Preston; hill in southwestern part of Middlebury, extending into Oxford; elevation, 660 feet... Derby.

Preston; hill in southwestern part of Kent; elevation, 1,300 feet.... Clove.

Prior; creek in western part of East Windsor, tributary to Connecticut River... Hartford.

Prospect; town in northern part of New Haven County; area, 16 square miles.
{ Waterbury. Meriden. Derby. New Haven. }

Prospect; village in central part of town of same name.............. Meriden.

Prospect; hill in Westport; elevation, 200 feet...................... Norwalk.

Prospect; hill in southwestern part of East Haven; elevation, 200 feet New Haven.

Prospect; hill in New Canaan; elevation, 437 feet .... Norwalk.

Prospect; hill in northeastern part of Pomfret; elevation, 680 feet .. Putnam.

Prospect; hill in northern part of Woodbridge; elevation, 475 feet .. Derby.

Prospect; hill in western part of Windham; elevation, 420 feet ..... Norwich.

Prospect; hill in southern part of Guilford; elevation, 161 feet...... Guilford.

Prospect; hill in central part of Preston; elevation, 320 feet........ Moosup.

Prospect; hill in northwestern part of Colchester; elevation, 480 feet. Gilead.

Prospect; mountain in eastern part of Salisbury; altitude, 1,475 feet. Cornwall.

Prospect; mountain in southwestern part of Litchfield; altitude, 1,365 feet .... New Milford.

Pudding; hill in northern part of Scotland; elevation, 540 feet ...... Norwich.

Purchase; brook in western part of Southbury, tributary to Housatonic River .... Danbury.

Names of sheets.

Purgatory; brook in eastern part of Watertown, tributary to branch of Naugatuck River.. Waterbury.

Putnam; town in eastern part of Windham County; area, 27 square miles... Putnam.

Putnam; principal village in town of same name, on Quinebaug River, and also on New York and New England R. R............. Putnam.

Putnam Heights; village in southern part of Putnam................ Putnam.

Quaddick; village in southeastern part of Thompson .... Putnam.

Quaduck; brook rising in eastern part of Killingly; flows south into Sterling and joins Moosup River..................................... Moosup.

Quaker; hill in eastern part of Waterford; elevation, 250 feet....... New London.

Quaker Farms; village in western part of Oxford.................... Derby.

Quaker Hill; village in northeastern part of Waterford.............. New London.

Quandunk; brook in southwestern part of Killingly, tributary to Quinebaug River.. Putnam.

Quarryville; village in northwestern part of Bolton................. Tolland.

Quassapaug pond in northwestern part of Middlebury.............. Waterbury.

Quiambog; cove, arm of Long Island Sound, indenting southwest coast of Stonington.. Stonington.

Quinebaug; village in northwestern part of Thompson, on New York and New England R. R.. Webster.

Quinebaug; pond in southwestern part of Killingly.................. Putnam.

Quinebaug; eastern branch of Thames River, rises in Massachusetts; flows south through entire eastern part of Connecticut into Thames River in southeastern part of Norwich.................... Norwich.

Quinebaug; river tributary to Shetucket River; rises in southern part of Massachusetts; flows south into Shetucket River in extreme northeastern part of Preston. { Webster. Putnam. Moosup. }

Quinnatisset; brook in southern part of Thompson, tributary to French River.. Putnam.

Quinnipiac; village in northern part of North Haven, on Quinnipiac River.. New Haven.

Quinnipiac; river rising in western part of New Britain; flows through Plainville, Southington, Cheshire, Meriden, Wallingford, and New Haven, into New Haven harbor. { New Haven. Meriden. }

Quonnipaug; mountain in northern part of Guilford; altitude, 532 feet. Guilford.

Quonnipaug; lake in northern part of Guilford...................... Guilford.

Rabbit; hill in southeastern part of Warren; elevation, 1,340 feet... New Milford.

Rabbit Rock; hill in southeastern part of North Haven; elevation, 340 feet... New Haven.

Race; brook rising in Woodbridge; flows south into Woppopaug River, in northwestern part of Orange............................... Derby.

Race; hill in western part of Madison; elevation, 322 feet........... Guilford.

Ragged; hill in Pomfret; elevation, 845 feet......................... Woodstock.

Ragged; mountain in western part of Berlin; altitude, 754 feet..... Meriden.

Ragland Hooppole; hill in southwestern part of Woodbury; elevation, 640 feet.. Waterbury.

Rainbow; village in northwestern part of Windsor, on Farmington River .... Hartford.

Ram; island off mouth of Norwalk River, in Long Island Sound .... Norwalk.

Rat; mountain in northeastern part of Washington; altitude, 1,120 feet.. New Milford.

Rattlesnake; hill in northeastern part of Somers, extending into Hampden, Mass... Palmer.

Names of sheets.

Rattlesnake; hill in northwestern part of North Canaan, having two peaks, the altitude of which are 960 and 980 feet, respectively .... Sheffield.

Rattlesnake; mountain in southern part of Farmington; altitude, 750 feet.. Meriden.

Rawson; village in northwestern part of Hampton.................... Woodstock.

Raymond; hill in northwestern part of Montville ; elevation, 588 feet .... New London.

Red; mountain in east central part of Cornwall; altitude, 1,660 feet. Cornwall.

Red City; village in central part of Oxford, on Little River......... Derby.

Redding; town in central part of Fairfield County; area, 13 square miles... Danbury.

Redding; village in central part of town of same name .... Danbury.

Redding Ridge; village in eastern part of Redding................ Danbury.

Reed Gap; hill in western part of Durham; elevation, 700 feet...... Guilford.

Reynolds Bridge; village in southeastern part of Thomaston on Naugatuck River, and on New York, New Haven and Hartford R. R... Waterbury.

Ridgebury; village in northwestern part of Ridgefield............. Carmel.

Ridgefield; town in western part of Fairfield County; area, 36 square miles.
{ Carmel.
{ Danbury.
{ Stamford.
{ Norwalk.

Ridgefield; principal village in south central part of town of same name.
{ Danbury.
{ Carmel.

Riga; lake in northwestern part of Salisbury .... Sheffield.

Riga; mountain in northwestern part of Salisbury; altitude, 1,900 feet. Sheffield.

Rigg Street; brook in northern part of Oxford, tributary to Jack Brook .... Derby.

Rimmon; brook rising in southeastern part of Beacon Falls; flows into Naugatuck River in northern part of Seymour .... Derby.

Rimmon; hill in southwestern part of Beacon Falls; elevation, 400 feet .... Derby.

Ritcher; mountain in south central part of North Stonington; altitude, 320 feet .... Stonington.

Riverside; village in southern part of Oxford .... Derby.

Riverside; village in southeastern part of Greenwich, on Coscob Harbor and on New York, New Haven and Hartford R. R............. Stamford.

Riverton; village in northwestern part of Barkhamsted .... Winsted.

Rixtown; mountain in Griswold, Preston and North Stonington, having four peaks, the altitudes of which are 440, 500, 520 and 600 feet, respectively .... Moosup.

Roaring; brook rising in northeastern part of Glastonbury; flows southwest into Connecticut River .... Middletown.

Roaring; brook rising in eastern part of Stafford, flowing into Willimantic River in northwestern part of Willington.
{ Woodstock.
{ Tolland.

Roaring; brook rising in southern part of Canton; flows south through Avon into Farmington River.................................. Granby.

Roast Meat; hill in southern part of Killingworth; elevation, 328 feet. Guilford.

Robertsville; village in southeastern part of Colebrook.............. Winsted.

Robinson; hill in western part of Hampton; elevation, 827 feet..... Woodstock.

Rock Fall; village in northeastern part of Middlefield, on New York, New Haven and Hartford R. R.................................... Middletown.

Rock Rimmon; mountain in southern part of Beacon Falls and in Seymour; altitude 570 feet... Derby.

Names of sheets.

Rockdale; village in southeastern part of Watertown, on Steel brook and also on New York, New Haven and Hartford R. R .... Waterbury.

Rockhouse; hill in southern part of Oxford; elevation, 590 feet..... Derby.

Rockland; village in northern part of Madison...................... Guilford.

Rockville; principal village of Vernon, located in northeastern part of town, on Hockanum River, also on New York and New England R. R... Tolland.

Rockwell; hill in southeastern part of Stafford; elevation, 933 feet.. Tolland.

Rocky; river, rises in central part of Sherman, flows south until it reaches east central part of New Fairfield, where it changes its course and flows north into Housatonic River in west central part of New Milford... New Milford.

Rocky; hill in western part of Bridgewater; elevation, 700 feet..... New Milford.

Rocky Glen; village in northern part of Newtown, on Pootatuck River... Danbury.

Rocky Hill; town in southern part of Hartford County; area, 19 square miles.. Middletown.

Rocky Hill; village in eastern part of town of same name on Connecticut River, also on New York, New Haven and Hartford R. R.. Middletown.

Rocky Neck; hill in southwestern part of East Lyme on coast; elevation, 120 feet... New London.

Roger; island off southern coast of Branford, in Long Island Sound.. New Haven.

Roger; lake in Lyme and Old Lyme................................. Saybrook.

Romford; village in northeastern part of Washington, on Shepaug River, also on Shepaug, Litchfield and Northern R. R .... New Milford.

Rooster; river rising in western part of Trumbull, flows south through Bridgeport, forming partial boundary between Bridgeport and Fairfield, into Long Island Sound .... Bridgeport.

Rose; hill in northwestern part of Ledyard; elevation, 280 feet...... New London.

Round; hill in northern part of Woodbridge; elevation, 590 feet..... Derby.

Round; hill in central part of Farmington; elevation, 320 feet...... Meriden.

Round; hill in southwestern part of Middletown; elevation, 650 feet. Middletown.

Round; hill in northwestern part of Greenwich; elevation, 551 feet.. Stamford.

Round; hill in eastern part of Easton; elevation, 595 feet........... Danbury.

Round; mountain in north central part of Ridgefield; altitude, 900 feet... Carmel.

Round; pond in western part of Ridgefield .... Carmel.

Roxbury; town in southern part of Litchfield County; area, 27 square miles .... New Milford.

Roxbury; principal village in town of same name .... New Milford.

Roxbury Falls; village in southwestern part of Roxbury on Shepaug River, also on Shepaug, Litchfield and Northern R. R.... New Milford.

Roxbury Station; village in western part of Roxbury on Shepaug River, also on Shepaug, Litchfield and Northern R. R........... New Milford.

Rucum; hill in southeastern part of Roxbury; elevation, 860 feet.... New Milford.

Sachem Head; point projecting from southern coast of town of Guilford into Long Island Sound...................................... Guilford.

Sachem Head Station; village in southern part of Guilford, on New York, New Haven and Hartford R. R .... Guilford.

Sadds Mills; village in northeastern part of East Windsor.......... Hartford.

Salem; town in western part of New London County; area, 30 square miles. { Gilead. Norwich. Saybrook. New London.

Names of sheets.

Salem; village in central part of town of same name................ Saybrook.

Salisbury; town in northwestern part of Litchfield County; area, { Sheffield.
61 square miles. { Cornwall.

Salisbury; village in central part of town of same name on Central
New England and Western R. R.................................... Cornwall.

Salmon; brook rising in northeastern part of Granby, tributary to
Farmington River.. Granby.

Salmon; creek rising in western part of Salisbury flowing into Housatonic River in southeastern part of Salisbury.................. Cornwall.

Salmon; river tributary to Connecticut River, rises in southern part
of Colchester, flows northwest, thence southwest through Colchester into Connecticut River................................... Gilead.

Salmon; cove at mouth of Salmon River, forms partial boundary between Haddam and East Haddam.................................. Saybrook.

Salt; island off southern coast of Westbrook in Long Island Sound.. Saybrook.

Saltonstall; lake forming partial boundary between East Haven and
Branford... New Haven.

Saltworks; bay off southern coast of Westbrook and Old Saybrook
in Long Island Sound.. Saybrook.

Sandford; mountain in southwestern part of Cheshire; altitude, 920
feet .... New Haven.

Sandy; point projecting from eastern coast of Orange into New
Haven Harbor.. New Haven.

Sandy; brook rising in western part of Sandisfield, Mass.; flows { Sandisfield.
southeast through Colebrook into Still River. { Winsted.

Sandy; point projecting from west coast of Waterford into Niantic
River... New London.

Sandy Hook; village in northern part of Newtown on Pootatuck
River... Danbury.

Sandy Hook Station; village in northern part of Newtown on Pootatuck River; also on New York and New England R. R......... Danbury.

Sanford Station; village in western part of Redding on Danbury
and Norwalk division of Housatonic R. R....................... Danbury.

Sargent; river; rises in central part of Bethany; flows south into
West River, in northeastern part of Woodbridge................. New Haven.

Satans Kingdom; hill in northeastern part of New Hartford; elevation, 110 feet.. Granby.

Saugatuck; village at mouth of Saugatuck River, in Westport, on
New York, New Haven and Hartford R. R....................... Norwalk.

Saugatuck; river; rises in southern part of Danbury; flows south- } Danbury.
east through Reading, Weston and Westport into Long Island { Norwalk.
Sound.

Savin Rock; village in southeastern part of Orange on Long Island
Sound .... New Haven.

Savin Rock; two islands lying off eastern coast of Orange, in Long
Island Sound .... New Haven.

Saybrook; town in southeastern part of Middlesex county; area, 15 { Guilford.
square miles. { Saybrook.

Saybrook; point projecting from southeastern coast of Old Saybrook
into Connecticut River... Saybrook.

Saybrook; jetties at entrance to Connecticut River in Long Island
Sound .... Saybrook.

Saybrook Junction; village in east central part of Old Saybrook, at
junction of Connecticut Valley and New York, New Haven and
Hartford R. R.. Saybrook.

Names of sheets.

Scantic; village in western part of East Windsor .... Hartford.

Scantic; river rising in northwest corner of Stafford, flows north into Hampden, Mass., and thence takes a westerly course through Somers, Enfield and East Windsor into Connecticut River. } Tolland. Hartford.

Scitico; village in eastern part of Enfield, on Scantic River, also on New York and New England R. R., Springfield Division........... Hartford.

Scotland; town in southwestern part of Windham County; area, 19 square miles .... Norwich.

Scotland; village in central part of town of same name............ Norwich.

Scotland Station; village in southwestern part of Scotland, on Shetucket River; also on New York and New England R. R .... Norwich.

Scott; cove indenting coast of Darien .... Norwalk.

Scott Ridge; mountain in western part of Ridgefield, having two peaks, the altitudes of which are 980 and 1,000 feet, respectively. Carmel.

Sea; hill in central part of North Branford; elevation, 380 feet...... New Haven.

Sebethe; river rising in western part of Berlin, flows east through Berlin, thence southeast, forming boundary between Berlin, Cromwell and Middletown, into Connecticut River. } Meriden. Middletown.

Second; hill in northern part of Bridgewater; elevation, 950 feet.. New Milford.

Selden; creek in western part of Lyme, tributary to Connecticut River... Saybrook.

Selden Neck; point extending from coast of Lyme into Connecticut River... Saybrook.

Seymour; town in western part of New Haven County; area, 15 square miles... Derby.

Seymour; principal village in town of same name, on Naugatuck River, also on branch New York, New Haven and Hartford R. R.... Derby.

Seymour; marshy point at mouth of Saugatuck River.............. Norwalk.

Shailorville; village in northeastern part of Haddam, on Connecticut River, and on Connecticut Valley Division New York, New Haven and Hartford R. R... Saybrook.

Shaker; pond in northern part of Enfield........................... Springfield.

Shaker; village in northeastern part of Enfield..................... Springfield.

Shaker Station; village in northeastern part of Enfield, on New York and New England R. R.. Springfield.

Sharon; town in western part of Litchfield County; area, 59 square miles... Carmel.

Sharon; principal village in town of same name..................... Cornwall.

Sharon Valley; village in northwestern part of Sharon............. Cornwall.

Sharpe; hill in Pomfret; elevation, 710 feet......................... Woodstock.

Shaw; cove extending from Thames River into east shore of New London.. New London.

Shaw; lake in northeastern part of East Haddam................... Gilead.

Sheffield; island off mouth of Norwalk River in Long Island Sound.. Norwalk.

Shelton; borough in Huntington, on Housatonic River, also on New Haven and Derby R. R.. Derby.

Shenipsit; lake forming partial boundary between Ellington, Tolland, and Vernon .... Tolland.

Shepaug; river rises in Litchfield, flows south through Washington and Roxbury, into Housatonic River, in western part of Southbury. } Danbury. New Milford.

Shepherd; pond in northwestern part of New Hartford............. Winsted.

Sherman; town in northern part of Fairfield County; area, 24 square miles. } Clove. New Milford.

Sherman; village in central part of town of same name............. New Milford.

Names of sheets.

Sherwood; point projecting into Long Island Sound from Westport. Norwalk.

Shetucket; river tributary to Quinebaug River, formed by Willimantic and Nachaug rivers, which meet in western part of Windham
and flow southeast through Sprague, forming boundary between
Norwich and Lisbon.. Norwich.

Shippan; point projecting from extreme southern coast of Stamford
into Long Island Sound.. Stamford.

Short Beach; village in southwestern part of Branford, on Long
Island Sound .... New Haven.

Shunock; river rising in western part of North Stonington, flows
southeast into Pawcatuck River .... Stonington.

Silvermine; hill in southwestern part of North Stonington; elevation, 340 feet .... Stonington.

Silvermine; river, right-hand branch of Norwalk River, in Fairfield
County.. Norwalk.

Simsbury; town in western part of Hartford County; area, 31 square
miles .... Granby.

Simsbury; village in eastern part of town of same name............ Granby.

Sixmile; brook in southern part of Oxford tributary to Eightmile
Brook .... Derby.

Skokorat; hill in northern part of Seymour and Bethany; elevation,
420 feet.. Derby.

Skungamaug; river tributary to Shetucket River rising in northern
part of Tolland, flows south through that town and through Coventry into Andover.. Tolland.

Slang; brook flowing into Long Island Sound from Darien.......... Norwalk.

Smith; cove extending from Niantic River into southeastern coast
of East Lyme .... New London.

Smith; cove extending from Niantic River into western coast of
Waterford .... New London.

Smith; cove extending from Thames River into northeastern coast of
Waterford .... New London.

Smith; cove on southern coast of Greenwich, in Long Island Sound.. Stamford.

Smith; pond in northern part of Watertown........................ Waterbury.

Snake Rock; hill in northeastern part of New Haven; elevation,
200 feet.. New Haven.

Snow; hill in Ashford; elevation, 1,213 feet .... Woodstock.

Soapstone; mountain in Somers and Ellington; altitude, 1,061 feet. Tolland.

Sodom; village in northern part of North Canaan, on Konkapot
River... Sheffield.

Sodom; brook in western part of Meriden, tributary to Quinnipiac
River... Meriden.

Somers; town in northwestern part of Tolland County; area, 28
square miles.
{ Springfield. Hartford. Palmer. Tolland.

Somers; village in central part of town of same name.............. Tolland.

Somerville; village in western part of Somers, on Scantic River..... Tolland.

Sound Beach; village in southeastern part of Greenwich, on New
York, New Haven and Hartford R. R............................... Stamford.

South; mountain in southern part of Bristol; altitude, 1,020 feet.... Meriden.

South; mountain extending from southwestern part of Berlin into
Meriden; altitude, 790 feet....................................... Meriden.

South; pond in northwestern part of Salisbury .... Sheffield.

Names of sheets.

South; cove from Connecticut River indenting southeastern coast of
Old Saybrook .... Saybrook.

South; cove from Connecticut River indenting southeastern coast of
Essex... Saybrook.

South Branch; river tributary to Harbor Brook, in eastern part of
Meriden .... Meriden.

South Britain; village in west central part of Southbury, on Pom- ⎰ Derby.
peraug River.   ⎱ Danbury.

South Canaan; village in western part of Canaan.................. Cornwall.

South Coventry; principal village in Coventry, located in southeastern part of the town, on Wamgumbaug Lake.................... Tolland.

South End; point projecting from southern part of East Haven into
Long Island Sound .... New Haven.

South Farms; village in northern part of Middletown .... Middletown.

South Glastonbury; village in southwestern part of Glastonbury, on
Roaring Brook.. Middletown.

South Kent; village in southwestern part of Kent, on Housatonic
R. R .... New Milford.

South Killingly; village in southeastern part of Killingly.......... Putnam.

South Lyme; village in southeastern part of Old Lyme .... Saybrook.

South Lyme Station; village in southeastern part of Old Lyme, on
New York, New Haven and Hartford R. R....................... Saybrook.

South Manchester; principal village of Manchester, located on south
branch Hockanum River and on New York and New England R. R. Hartford.

South Meriden; village in southwestern part of Meriden on Quinnipiac River... Meriden.

South Norfolk; village in southern part of Norfolk .... Winsted.

South Norwalk; city in Fairfield County, at mouth of Norwalk River
on New York, New Haven and Hartford R. R.................... Norwalk.

South Spectacle; pond in eastern part of Kent..................... New Milford.

South Weathersfield; village in southeastern part of Wethersfield
on New York, New Haven and Hartford R. R.................... Middletown.

South Willington; village in southwestern part of Willington..... Tolland.

South Wilton; village in Wilton .... Norwalk.

South Windham; village in southwestern part of Windham, on Shetucket River, also on New London Northern R. R .... Norwich.

South Windsor; town in eastern part of Hartford County; area, 30
square miles.. Hartford.

South Windsor; village in southwest part of town of same name... Hartford.

South Woodstock; village in southeastern part of Woodstock..... Putnam.

⎧ New Milford.
Southbury; town in northwestern part of New Haven County; area, ⎬ Waterbury.
40 square miles.   ⎪ Danbury.
⎩ Derby.

Southbury; village in central part of town of same name .... Derby.

Southford; village in southeastern part of Southbury; also on New
York and New England R. R .... Derby.

Southington; town in southwestern part of Hartford Country; area,
38 square miles .... Meriden.

Southington; borough in town of same name on Quinnipiac River;
also on New York, New Haven and Hartford R. R .... Meriden.

Southington Road Station; village in northeastern part of Cheshire
on Meriden and Waterbury R. R............................... Meriden.

Southport; village in Fairfield.................................... Norwalk.

Spalding; pond in southeastern part of North Stonington........... Stonington.

Names of sheets.

Spaulding; pond in eastern part of Norwich........................ Norwich.

Spectacle; island off southern coast of Branford in Long Island Sound. New Haven.

Spooner; hill in western part of Kent; elevation, 1,100 feet........... New Milford.

Spooner; hill in southwestern part of Kent; elevation, 780 feet..... New Milford.

Sprague; town in northern part of New London County; area, 14 square miles.. Norwich.

Sprain; brook rising in eastern part of Washington, flows into { Waterbury.
Pomperaug river in central part of Woodbury. { New Milford.

Spring; hill in Mansfield... Woodstock.

Sprite; island in Long Island Sound, part of Norwalk............... Norwalk.

Spruce; brook in southwestern part of Naugatuck tributary to Naugatuck River... Derby.

Spruce; brook in western part of Southbury tributary to Transylvania brook.. Danbury.

Spy Rock; hill in northwestern part of Griswold; elevation, 360 feet.. Moosup.

Squabble; brook in northern part of Canaan tributary to Konkapot River.. Sheffield.

Squantuck; village in southwestern part of Seymour on Housatonic River.. Derby.

Squantz; pond in northern part of New Fairfield.................. New Milford.

Square; pond on southwestern boundary of line of Stafford, being partly in Ellington and partly in Stafford....................... Tolland.

Square Pond; brook rising in northwestern part of Stafford tributary to Willimantic River.. Tolland.

Squaw Rock; island off southern coast of Branford in Long Island Sound.. New Haven.

Staddle; hill in western part of Middletown; elevation, 180 feet.... Middletown.

Stafford; town in northern part of Tolland County; area, 42 square miles. { Palmer. / Brookfield. / Tolland. / Woodstock.

Stafford; village in eastern part of Stafford on Furnace brook....... Tolland.

Stafford Springs; borough in Stafford on Willimantic River, and on New London Northern R. R..................................... Tolland.

Staffordville; village in eastern part of Stafford.................... Tolland.

Stamford; town in southwestern part of Fairfield County; area, 38 square miles.. Stamford.

Stamford; borough in town of same name on Long Island Sound, and also on New York, New Haven and Hartford R. R.............. Stamford.

Stamford; cove from Long Island Sound indenting southern coast of Stamford... Stamford.

Stanwich; village in northwestern part of Greenwich.............. Stamford.

State Line; pond in northern part of Stafford..................... Palmer.

State Line; village in western part of Salisbury on Central New England and Western R. R.. Cornwall.

State Prison; village in northeastern part of Wethersfield.......... Middletown.

Steel; brook rising in northern part of Watertown, flows southeast through Watertown into Naugatuck River in northwestern part of Waterbury... Waterbury.

Stepney; village in southern part of Monroe, on Housatonic River.. { Danbury. { Derby.

Sterling; town in southeastern part of Windham County; area, 27 square miles. { Putnam. { Moosup.

Names of sheets.

Sterling; village in western part of town of same name .... Moosup.

Sterling Station; village in central part of Sterling on Moosup River, also on Providence division New York and New England R. R ... Moosup.

Stevenson; village in northeastern part of Monroe on New Haven and Derby R. R.. Derby.

Stewart; hill in central part of North Stonington; elevation, 500 feet. Stonington.

Stickney; hill in Union; elevation, 1,200 feet .... Woodstock.

Still; river rises in western part of Danbury, flows northeast through ⎰ Danbury. Danbury and Brookfield, into Housatonic River in western part ⎱ Carmel. of New Milford. ⎱ New Milford.

Still; river rises in eastern part of Torrington, flows north through that town and Winchester and southeast corner of Colebrook into West Branch of Farmington River in northwest part of Barkhamsted .... Winsted.

Still; river rising in southwest part of Woodstock, tributary to Natchaug River .... Woodstock.

Stillman; pond in eastern part of Bridgeport .... Bridgeport.

Stillmanville; village in eastern part of Stonington on Pawcatuck River... Stonington.

Stillriver; village in southern part of New Milford on Housatonic River... New Milford.

Stoddard; hill in northwestern part of Ledyard; elevation, 200 feet. New London.

Stone; hill in northeastern part of Griswold; elevation, 500 feet .... Moosup.

Stone House; brook in Chaplin tributary to Natchaug River....... Woodstock.

Stonington; town in southeastern part of New London County; area, 42 square miles... Stonington.

Stonington; borough in town of same name on Long Island Sound.. Stonington.

Stonington; point projecting from southern coast of Stonington into Long Island Sound... Stonington.

Stonington; harbor, arm of Long Island Sound indenting southern coast of Stonington... Stonington.

Stony Creek; village in southeastern part of Branford, on Long Island Sound .... New Haven.

Stony; brook rises in northwestern part of Montville, flows southeast into Thames River .... New London.

Stony; brook in western part of Waterford tributary to Niantic River. New London.

Stony; brook rises in western part of Suffield, flows southwest through Suffield into Connecticut River................................... Hartford,

Stony; brook, right branch of Saugatuck River, in Westport .... Norwalk.

Stony; brook in southern part of Stonington, flowing into Stonington Harbor .... Stonington.

Storrs; village in northwestern part of Mansfield................... Tolland.

Stoughton; brook in western part of South Windsor, branch of Connecticut River .... Hartford.

Straitsville; village in southeastern part of Naugatuck .... Derby,

Stratford; town in southeastern part of Fairfield County; area, 39 ⎰ Derby. square miles. ⎱ Bridgeport.

Stratford; village in southeastern part of town of same name on Housatonic River, also on New York, New Haven and Hartford R. R.. Bridgeport.

Stratford; point projecting from southeastern coast of Stratford into Long Island Sound.. Bridgeport.

Strawberry; hill in central part of Durham; elevation, 366 feet..... Guilford.

Strongtown; village in northeastern part of Southbury............. Derby.

Sturgis Ridge; hill in Wilton.................................... Norwalk.

Names of sheets.

Sucker; brook in western part of East Haddam, tributary to Connecticut River... Saybrook.

Suffield; town in northern part of Hartford County; area, 44 square miles.
{ Granville.
Granby.
Springfield.
Hartford.

Suffield; village in eastern part of town of same name .... Hartford.

Sugar; brook in western part of Plainfield, flows north into Quinebaug River... Moosup.

Sugar Loaf; hill in northwestern part of Guilford; elevation, 514 feet. Guilford.

Sumac; island off southern coast of Branford in Long Island Sound. New Haven.

Summit; village in northwestern part of Cheshire .... Meriden.

Susquetonscut; brook rising in western part of Franklin, flows south into Yantic River in northeast part of Bozrah .... Norwich.

Swantown; hill in western part of North Stonington, having three peaks, altitude of which are 420, 420, and 440 feet, respectively.. Stonington.

Sweet; hill in northern part of Lebanon; elevation, 641 feet........ Norwich.

Swift Bridge; village in southwestern part of Cornwall, on Housatonic River, also on Housatonic R. R .... Cornwall.

Taft Station; village in eastern part of Norwich, on Shetucket River, also on Norwich and Worcester R. R.............................. Norwich.

Taftville; village in northeastern part of Norwich, on Shetucket River. Norwich.

Talcott; range of mountains extending through towns of East Granby, Simsbury, Bloomfield, Avon, West Hartford, and Farmington.... Granby.

Talcottville; village in southwestern part of Vernon, on New York and New England R. R.. Tolland.

Tancanhoosen; river rising in western part of Tolland, flows southwesterly through Vernon into Hockanum River................... Tolland.

Tanvat; brook in western part of Waterbury, tributary to Welton Brook .... Waterbury.

Tariffville; village in northeastern part of Simsbury, on Tunxis or Farmington River, also on New York, New Haven and Hartford R. R., Northampton division.. Granby.

Tashua; hill in western part of Trumbull; elevation, 620 feet........ Danbury,

Tatetuck; brook in eastern part of Easton, tributary to Mill River. Danbury.

Tatnic; brook rising in southwestern part of Brooklyn, flows into Blackwell Brook in northeast part of Canterbury................. Putnam.

Tatnic; hill in southwestern part of Brooklyn, having two peaks, altitude of each being 540 feet..................................... Putnam.

Taugwank; hill in central part of Stonington; elevation, 180 feet... Stonington.

Taunton; hill in western part of Newtown; elevation, 832 feet...... Danbury.

Taunton; pond in western part of Newtown......................... Danbury.

Taunton Rock; island off southwestern coast of Branford, in Long Island Sound.. New Haven.

Tavern; island off coast of Norwalk................................. Norwalk.

Tenmile; hill in northwestern part of Sherman; elevation, 950 feet. Clove.

Tenmile; river rising in northeastern part of Prospect, and flowing northeast through northwestern Cheshire into Quinnipiac River, in southern part of Southington .... Meriden.

Terryville; village in eastern part of Plymouth, on New York and New England R. R.. Meriden.

Terryville; village in eastern part of Plymouth, on Pequabuck River. Waterbury.

Names of sheets.

Thames; river formed by two branches, the Quinnebaug and Yantic Rivers. These two rivers meet in southeastern part of Norwich and form the Thames, which flows south, forming boundary between Ledyard, Waterford, and Groton.......................... Norwich.

Thatchbed; island off eastern coast of Essex, in Connecticut River.... Saybrook.

Thayer; brook in western part of Kent, tributary to Housatonic River.. New Milford.

Thimble; group of islands off southern coast of Branford, in Long Island Sound... New Haven.

Thomaston; town in southeastern part of Litchfield County; area, 12 square miles.. Waterbury.

Thomaston; principal village in town of same name, on Naugatuck River, and also on New York, New Haven and Hartford R. R...... Waterbury.

Thomasville; village in southeastern part of Norwich, on Thames River, also on New London Northern R. R....................... Norwich.

Thompson; town in northeastern part of Windham County; area, 50 ⌠ Webster. square miles.   ⌡ Putnam.

Thompson; village in south central part of town of same name...... Putnam.

Thompson Station; village in south central part of Thompson, on New York and New England R. R.............................. Putnam.

Thompsonville; village in western part of Enfield, on Connecticut ⌠ Hartford. River, and on New York, New Haven and Hartford R. R.   ⌡ Springfield.

Three Notches; three small hills in western part of Durham, altitudes of which are 600, 620, and 640 feet, respectively............ Guilford.

Titicus; village in central part of Ridgefield........................ Carmel.

Titicus; mountain in southwestern part of New Fairfield .... Carmel.

Titus; mountain in northeastern part of Cornwall; altitude, 1,500 feet .... Cornwall.

Toby; mountain in southwestern part of Plymouth; altitude, 893 feet .... Waterbury.

Toby Rock; mountain in eastern part of Oxford, extending into Beacon Falls; altitude, 730 feet...................................... Derby.

Tobey; pond in western part of Norfolk .... Winsted.

Todd; hill in northwestern part of Bethlehem; elevation, 1,140 feet. Waterbury.

Todd Hollow; brook rising in central part of Plymouth, flows into Hancock brook .... Waterbury.

Toll Bridge; brook in eastern part of Newtown, tributary to Housatonic River.. Danbury.

Tolland; town in central part of Tolland County; area, 42 square miles .... Tolland.

Tolland; village of town of same name............................. Tolland.

Tolland Station; village in western part of Willington, on Willimantic River, and on New London Northern R. R..................... Tolland.

Tolles; village in southeastern part of Plymouth, on Hancock Brook, and on New York and New England R. R........................ Waterbury.

Tom; mountain in northwestern part of East Haddam; altitude, 312 feet .... Saybrook.

Tom; mountain in Morris and Washington; altitude, 1,325 feet...... New Milford.

Tom; mountain in central part of New Milford; altitude, 1,100 feet.. New Milford.

Tom; mountain in northeastern part of Salisbury, having two peaks. Sheffield.

Torringford; village in eastern part of Torrington .... Winsted.

Torrington; town in central part of Litchfield County; area, 38 square miles .... Winsted.

Names of sheets.

Torrington; borough in town of same name, reached by New York, New Haven and Hartford R. R. ... Winsted.

Totoket; village in southwestern part of North Branford ... New Haven.

Totoket; mountain in northwestern part of Guilford, greatest elevation being 780 feet ... Guilford.

Towantic; village in northeastern part of Oxford, on New York and New England R. R. ... Derby.

Towantic; brook in northeastern part of Oxford, tributary to Little River ... Derby.

Towantic; hill in northeastern part of Oxford, having two peaks, altitude of each being 700 feet ... Derby.

Tower; hill in southeastern part of Killingworth, extending into Saybrook; elevation, 382 feet ... Guilford.

Tower; hill in Chaplin; elevation, 500 feet ... Woodstock.

Town; hill in eastern part of Warren; elevation, 1,340 feet ... New Milford.

Town Farm; brook in southern part of New Milford, tributary to Housatonic River; forms partial boundary between New Milford and Bridgewater ... New Milford.

Town Plot; hill in southwestern part of Waterbury; altitude, 668 feet ... Waterbury.

Towner; hill in eastern part of Sherman; elevation, 920 feet ... New Milford.

Trading; cove extending from Thames River into southeastern coast of Norwich ... New London.

Trading Cove; brook forming boundary between Bozrah, Norwich, and Montville, tributary to Thames River ... Norwich.

Transylvania; brook rising in southeastern part of Roxbury, flows into Pomperaug River, in central part of Southbury ... Danbury.

Trout; brook in central part of Orange, tributary to Indian River ... Derby.

Trout; brook in southwestern part of Washington, tributary to Shepaug River ... New Milford.

Trout; brook in eastern part of Westbrook, tributary to Patchogue River ... Saybrook.

Trout; brook rising in western part of West Hartford, tributary to Connecticut River ... Granby.

Trumbull; town in eastern part of Fairfield County; area, 24 square miles. { Danbury. Derby. Bridgeport.

Trumbull; village in southern part of town of same name, on Housatonic R. R. ... Bridgeport.

Tunxis River. (*See* Farmington River.)

Turkey; brook in southern part of Watertown, tributary to Steel Brook ... Waterbury.

Turkey; hill in western part of Berlin; elevation, 385 feet ... Meriden.

Turkey; hill in southeastern part of Haddam; elevation, 485 feet ... Guilford.

Turkey; hill in western part of Orange and Milford; elevation, 140 feet ... Derby.

Turner; ridge in Wilton ... Norwalk.

Turnerville; village in southeastern part of Hebron, on New York, New Haven and Hartford R. R ... Gilead.

Tixis; island off southern coast of Madison, in Long Island Sound ... Guilford.

Tweed; island off southern coast of Greenwich, in Long Island Sound. Stamford.

Twin; two islands in Pocotopaug Lake, in eastern part of Chatham. Middletown.

Twin; two lakes in northeastern part of Salisbury ... Sheffield.

Names of sheets.

Twin Lakes; village in northeastern part of Salisbury, on Twin
Lakes, also on Connecticut Western R. R........................ Sheffield.

Twomile; brook rising in eastern Ansonia, flows southwest into
Housatonic River, forming partial boundary between Derby and
Orange .... Derby.

Two Tree; island off southwestern coast of Waterford, in Long Island
Sound .... New London.

Tylerville; pond in western part of Goshen.......................... Cornwall.

Tylerville; village in southeastern part of Haddam.................. Saybrook.

Umpawaug; pond in northwestern part of Redding................. Danbury.

Umpog; creek rising in eastern part of Danbury, forming boundary
between Bethel and Danbury, flowing into Still River in east central part of Danbury... Danbury.

Uncasville; village in southeastern part of Montville............... New London.

Union; town in northeastern part of Tolland County; area, 29 square { Brookfield.
miles.   { Woodstock.

Union; village in town of same name................................. Woodstock.

Union City; village in northern part of Naugatuck, on Naugatuck
River and on New York, New Haven and Hartford R. R.......... Waterbury.

Unionville; village in northwestern part of Farmington............. Granby.

Upper Kohanza; pond in northwestern part of Danbury............. Danbury.

Upper Stepney; village in western part of Monroe.................. Danbury.

Upper White; hill in northern part of Huntington; elevation, 600
feet .... Derby.

Utley; hill in Pomfret; elevation, 748 feet........................... Woodstock.

Valley Forge; village in northeastern part of Weston............... Danbury.

Vernon; town in western part of Tolland County; area, 19 square { Tolland.
miles.   { Hartford.

Vernon; village in southwestern part of town of same name........ Tolland.

Vernon Center; village in central part of Vernon................... Tolland.

Versailles; village in western part of Lisbon, on Shetucket River... Norwich.

Versailles Station; village in western part of Lisbon, on New York
and New England R. R., Providence Division .... Norwich.

Vinegar; hill in western part of Ledyard; elevation, 365 feet........ New London.

Voluntown; town in northeastern part of New London County; area,
41 square miles... Moosup.

Voluntown; village in west central part of town of same name, on
Pachaug River... Moosup.

Wachocastinook; creek, rises in western part of Salisbury, flows into
Salmon Creek.. Sheffield.

Wallingford; town in eastern part of New Haven County; area, 43 { Meriden.
square miles.   { New Haven.
                                                                     { Guilford.

Wallingford; borough in central part of town of same name, on Quinnipiac River and on New York, New Haven and Hartford R. R .. New Haven.

Walnut; hill in western part of Madison; elevation, 365 feet......... Guilford.

Walnut Tree; hill in eastern part of Southbury; elevation, 790 feet. Derby.

Walnut Tree; hill in western part of Huntington; elevation, 520 feet. Derby.

Walkley; hill in northern part of Haddam; elevation, 230 feet....... Guilford.

Wamgumbaug; lake in the southeastern part of Coventry.......... Tolland

Wamphassuc Neck; strip of land projecting from southern coast of
Stonington into Stonington Harbor and into Long Island Sound.. Stonington.

Wanzer; hill in southern part of Sherman; elevation, 1,140 feet..... New Milford.

Names of sheets.

Wappaguia; brook in northern part of Pomfret, tributary to Mash-
ammoquet Brook.. Putnam.

Wapping; village in southern part of South Windsor............... Hartford.

Waramaug; lake on western boundary, between Warren and Washington.. New Milford.

Warehouse Point; village in East Windsor, in northwest part, on
Connecticut River.. Hartford.

Warren; town in western part of Litchfield County; area, 28 square (Cornwall.
miles.   (New Milford.

Warren; village in central part of town of same name............... New Milford.

Warrenville; village in Ashford................................... Woodstock.

Wash; brook in Bloomfield, tributary to Hog River................. Hartford.

Washington; town in southern part of Litchfield County; area, 39
square miles... New Milford.

Washington Green; village in south central part of Washington... New Milford.

Washington Station; village in central part of Washington, on Shepaug River, and on Shepaug, Litchfield and Northern R. R ...... New Milford.

Watchaug; brook rising in Hampden, Mass., flows south into Scantic
Brook, in northern part of Somers.............................. Palmer.

Water House; pond in northeastern part of Chester............... Saybrook.

Waterbury; town in northern part of New Haven County; area, (Waterbury.
29 square miles.   (Meriden.

Waterbury; city in central part of town of same name, on Naugatuck
River.. Waterbury.

Waterford; town in southern part of New London County; area, 39
square miles... New London.

Waterford; village in eastern part of town of same name, on Thames
River, and on New London and Northern R. R................... New London.

Waterford; island off southwestern coast of Waterford, in Long
Island Sound.. New London.

Watertown; town in southeastern part of Litchfield County; area,
30 square miles... Waterbury.

Watertown; village in town of same name, on Watertown Branch
New York, New Haven and Hartford R. R....................... Waterbury.

Waterville; village in northern part of Waterbury, on New York and
New England R. R... Waterbury.

Wattles; pond in southwestern part of Watertown................. Waterbury.

Wauregan; village in northwestern part of Plainfield, on Quinebaug
River.. Moosup.

Waweous; hill in southwestern part of Norwich; elevation, 500 feet. Norwich.

Weatogue; village in southeastern part of Simsbury, on New York,
New Haven and Hartford R. R., Northampton Division.......... Granby.

Webster; point on southeastern coast of Madison, projecting into
Long Island Sound.. Guilford.

Weekeepeemee; river rising in northwestern part of Bethlehem,
flows south through same town into Pomperaug River, in northwestern part of Woodbury..................................... Waterbury.

Welches; point projecting from southern coast of Milford into Long
Island Sound... Bridgeport.

Wellsville; village in central part of New Milford, on East Aspetuck
River.. New Milford.

Welton; brook in western part of Waterbury, tributary to Hop Brook. Waterbury.

Wepawaug; river rising in northern part of Woodbridge and flowing (Derby.
south through Orange and Milford into Long Island Sound.   (Bridgeport.

Wequetequock; village in southern part of Stonington, on Wequetequock River .... Stonington.

Wequetequock; river in southern part of Stonington; flows into Little Narragansett Bay .... Stonington.

West; river rising in northwest part of Guilford; flows south into Guilford Harbor, Long Island Sound............................. Guilford.

West; river rising in Bethany; flows south through Woodbridge and New Haven into New Haven Harbor................................ New Haven.

West; pond in west central part of Guilford........................... Guilford.

West Ashford; village in Ashford .... Woodstock.

West Aspetuck; river rising in southeastern part of Kent; flows south and joins the East Aspetuck, and together they flow into Housatonic River, in central part of New Milford................. New Milford.

West Avon; village in central part of Avon .... Granby.

West Cheshire; village in west central part of Cheshire, on Northampton division, New York, New Haven and Hartford R. R. { New Haven. Meriden.

West Cornwall; village in western part of Cornwall, on Housatonic River and on Housatonic R. R..................................... Cornwall.

West Goshen; village in western part of Goshen .... Cornwall.

West Granby; village in south central part of Granby............... Granby.

West Hartford; town in central part of Hartford County; area, 21 square miles. { Granby. Hartford. Meriden. Middletown.

West Hartford; village in eastern part of town of same name....... Hartford.

West Hartland; village in central part of Hartland................. Granville.

West Haven; borough in eastern part of Orange, on New Haven Harbor and on New York, New Haven and Hartford R. R .... New Haven.

West Norfolk; village in northwestern part of Norfolk .... Sandisfield.

West Norwalk; village in western part of town of Norwalk........ Norwalk.

West Peak; hill in northwestern part of Meriden; elevation, 1,007 feet Meriden.

West Pudding; village in northwestern part of Redding on Danbury and Norwalk division of Housatonic R. R......................... Danbury.

West Rock; ridge of mountains forming boundary between Hampden and Woodbridge, and extending into northwest part of New Haven; greatest elevation, 670 feet.............................. New Haven.

West Rock; hill in northwest part of New Haven; elevation, 405 feet... New Haven.

West Side; pond in western part of Goshen .... Cornwall.

West Stafford; village in western part of Stafford on Square Pond Brook .... Tolland.

West Stratford; village, part of Bridgeport city, situated on Long Island Sound .... Bridgeport.

West Street; village in northern part of Vernon.................... Tolland.

West Suffield; village in west central part of Suffield .... Hartford.

West Sugar Loaf; hill in northwestern part of Guilford; elevation, 480 feet... Guilford.

West Thompson; village in southwestern part of Thompson, on Quinebaug River .... Putnam.

West Torrington; village in western part of Torrington on Naugatuck River.. Winsted.

West Winsted; village in eastern part of Winchester, on Mad River and on Central New England and Western R. R .... Winsted.

West Woodstock; village in Woodstock .... Woodstock.

Names of sheets.

Westbrook; town in southern part of Middlesex County; area, 19 square miles. { Guilford. Saybrook.

Westbrook; village in southern part of town of same name, on Patchogue River and on New York, New Haven and Hartford R. R.. Saybrook.

Westbrook; harbor off southern coast of Westbrook............... Saybrook.

Westchester; village in southwestern part of Colchester .... Gilead.

Westchester Station; village in northwestern part of Colchester, on New York, New Haven and Hartford R. R .... Gilead.

Westcott; cove, arm of Long Island Sound, indenting southern coast of Stamford... Stamford.

Westfield; village in northwestern part of Middletown .... Middletown.

Westfield Station; village in western part of Cromwell, on Sebethe River and on Meriden, Waterbury and Connecticut River R. R... Middletown.

Westford; village in Ashford .... Woodstock.

Westford; hill in Ashford; elevation, 957 feet .... Woodstock.

Westminster; village in western part of Canterbury .... Norwich.

Weston; town in western part of Fairfield County; area, 20 square miles. { Danbury. Norwalk.

Weston; village in town of same name .... Norwalk.

Westport; town in southern part of Fairfield County; area, 22 square miles .... Norwalk.

Westport; village in town of same name .... Norwalk.

Westville; village in western part of New Haven................... New Haven.

Wetaug; village in northeastern part of Salisbury .... Sheffield.

Wethersfield; town in southern part of Hartford County; area, 14 square miles .... Middletown.

Wethersfield; village in eastern part of town of same name, on Valley division New York, New Haven and Hartford R. R............... Middletown.

Wewaka; brook rising in central part of Bridgewater; flows south into Housatonic River... New Milford.

Whetstone; brook in Killingly....................................... Putnam.

Whigville; village in southeastern part of Burlington .... Meriden.

Whits; pond in eastern part of Goshen .... Winsted.

White Deer Rocks; hill in southeastern part of Woodbury; elevation, 736 feet.. Waterbury.

White Rocks; several hills in northeastern part of Middletown, one having a height of 500 feet and another about 560 feet .... Middletown.

Whiting; river rising in southern part of New Marlboro, Mass.; flows south into Blackberry River in central part of North Canaan .... Sheffield.

Whitney; lake in southeastern part of Hamden...................... New Haven.

Whitneyville; village in Hamden, on boundary between Hamden and New Haven, and on Northampton division New York, New Haven and Hartford R. R .... New Haven.

Wig; hill in central part of Chester; elevation, 515 feet............. Saybrook.

Williamsville; village in northwestern part of Killingly, on Quinebaug River... Putnam.

Willimantic; borough in western part of Windham, on Willimantic River.. Norwich.

Willimantic; river tributary to Shetucket; has its source in northern part of Stafford, flows southerly through Stafford, and forms boundary line between Ellington, Tolland, and Willington, and Coventry and Mansfield.. Tolland.

Willington; town in eastern part of Tolland County; area, 35 square miles. { Tolland. Woodstock.

Bull. 117——5

Names of sheets.

Willington; village in south central part of town of same name..... Tolland.

Willow; island in Connecticut River at mouth of Sebethe River.... Middletown.

Willow; brook in central part of East Hartford, tributary to Connecticut River.. Hartford.

Wilson; village in northeastern part of Hartford, on New York, New Haven and Hartford R. R .... Hartford.

Wilson; point projecting into Long Island Sound from Norwalk.... Norwalk.

Wilsonville; village in north central part of Thompson, on French River and on New York and New England R. R.................... Webster.

Wilton; town in western part of Fairfield County; area, 28 square { Danbury.
miles. { Norwalk.

Wilton; village in town of same name................................. Norwalk.

Winchester; town in northeastern part of Litchfield County; area, 36 square miles... Winsted.

Winchester; village in southwestern part of town of same name.... Winsted.

Windemere; village in southwestern part of Ellington, on Springfield division New York and New England R. R .... Tolland.

Windham; town in southwestern part of Windham County; area, 26 square miles.. Norwich.

Windham Center; village in central part of Windham.............. Norwich.

Windsor; town in northern part of Hartford County; area, 31 square miles... Hartford.

Windsor; village in eastern part of town of same name, on New York, New Haven and Hartford R. R., and on Farmington River....... Hartford.

Windsor Locks; town in northern part of Hartford County; area, 10 square miles .... Hartford.

Windsor Locks; village in eastern part of town of same name, on Connecticut River and on New York, New Haven and Hartford R. R., Hartford Division....................................... Hartford.

Windsorville; village in southeastern part of East Windsor,......... Hartford.

Winnipauk; village in Norwalk....................................... Norwalk.

Winsted; borough in east central part of Winchester................ Winsted.

Wintechog; hill in western part of North Stonington, having two peaks, altitude of each being 420 feet............................ Stonington.

Wintergreen; lake in southwestern part of Hamden .... New Haven.

Winthrop; village in western part of Saybrook .... Saybrook.

Winthrop; cove extending from Thames River into eastern shore New London .... New London.

Winthrop; point projecting from New London into Thames River... New London.

Wolcott; town in northern part of New Haven County; area, 21 { Waterbury.
square miles. { Meriden.

Wolcott; village in central part of town of same name .... Meriden.

Womenshenuk; brook rising in southern part of Kent, flows south into Housatonic River, in northwestern part of New Milford...... New Milford.

Wononpakok; lake in southwestern part of Salisbury.............. Cornwall.

Wononscopomus; lake in southwestern part of Salisbury .... Cornwall.

Wood; river heading in southwestern part of Sterling, flowing southeast into Rhode Island .... Moosup.

Wood; creek in western part of Bethlehem, tributary to Weekeepeemee River .... Waterbury.

Wood; creek rising in northern part of Danbury, flowing into Rocky River, in eastern part of New Fairfield............................ Danbury.

Woodbridge; town in western part of New Haven County; area, 21 { Derby.
square miles. { New Haven.

Names of sheets.

Woodbridge; village in central part of town of same name .... Derby.

Woodbury; town in southern part of Litchfield County; area, 36 { New Milford.
square miles. { Woodbury.

Woodbury; village in south central part of town of same name..... Waterbury.

Woodchuck; hill in southwestern part of Canterbury; elevation, 500
feet .... Norwich.

Woodruff; hill in northern part of Oxford, extending into Middlebury;
elevation, 880 feet.. Derby.

Wooster; brook rising in western part of Waterbury, tributary to
Hop Brook .... Waterbury.

Wooster; mountain in northern part of Ridgefield; greatest elevation, 1,060 feet .... Danbury.

Woodstock; town in northern part of Windham County; area, 62
square miles.
{ Brookfield.
{ Webster.
{ Woo…stock.
{ Putnam.

Woodstock; village in southeastern part of town of same name.... Putnam.

Woodstock; pond in southeastern part of Woodstock.............. Putnam.

Woodstock Valley; village in Woodstock.......................... Woodstock.

Woodville; village in northeastern part of Washington, on West
Branch of Shepaug River...................................... New Milford.

Wopopaug. (*See* Wepawaug.)

Wormwood; hill in Mansfield; elevation, 653 feet.................. Woodstock.

Worton; brook tributary to Quinnipiac River, forms boundary between Wallingford and North Haven........................... New Haven.

Wungum; lake in northeastern part of Canaan..................... Cornwall.

Wyassup; lake in north central part of North Stonington.......... Stonington.

Yalesville; village in northwestern part of Wallingford, on Quinnipiac River... New Haven.

Yantic; village in western part of Norwich, on Yantic River, and on
New London Northern R. R...................................... Norwich.

Yantic; western branch of Thames River, rises in Lebanon and flows
southeast through Bozrah into Thames River, in southeastern part
of Norwich.. Norwich.

Yellow Mill; pond in southeastern part of Bridgeport.............. Bridgeport.

Zoar Bridge; village in western part of Oxford, on Housatonic River. Derby.

O

UNITED STATES GEOLOGICAL SURVEY

J. W. POWELL, DIRECTOR

A

GEOGRAPHIC DICTIONARY

OF

RHODE ISLAND

BY

HENRY GANNETT

WASHINGTON

GOVERNMENT PRINTING OFFICE

1894

LETTER OF TRANSMITTAL.

DEPARTMENT OF THE INTERIOR,
U. S. GEOLOGICAL SURVEY,
DIVISION OF GEOGRAPHY,
Washington, D. C., January 15, 1894.

SIR: I have the honor to transmit herewith for publication a geographic dictionary of Rhode Island.

Very respectfully,

HENRY GANNETT,
Chief Topographer.

Hon. J. W. POWELL,
Director U. S. Geological Survey.

A GEOGRAPHIC DICTIONARY OF RHODE ISLAND.

By HENRY GANNETT.

The Geographic Dictionary of Rhode Island, which constitutes this bulletin, is designed to aid in finding any geographic feature upon the atlas sheets of that State published by the U. S. Geological Survey. It contains all the names given upon those sheets, and no other. Under each name is a brief statement showing the feature it designates and its location, and opposite to it is the name of the atlas sheet or sheets upon which it is to be found.

The atlas sheets upon which the State is represented are the result of a survey made at the joint expense of the U. S. Geological Survey and the State of Rhode Island. The scale upon which the sheets are published is 1:62500: that is, a distance of 62,500 inches upon the ground, or very nearly 1 mile, is represented by 1 inch upon the map. Relief, or variation of elevation, is represented by contour lines or lines of equal elevation above mean sea level, these contour lines being at vertical intervals of 20 feet; so that each successive contour indicates a level 20 feet higher than the one below it. Upon the map all water bodies, that is, bays, ponds, rivers, etc., are represented in blue; the contour lines representing the relief, together with the figures showing absolute elevations, are printed in brown; and the lettering and all lines indicating the works of man are printed in black.

The area of the State is represented upon 15 sheets, each sheet comprising 15 minutes of latitude by 15 minutes of longitude. Each sheet, therefore, includes about 17½ miles from north to south and about 13 miles from east to west. Of these sheets only 4 lie entirely or virtually within the State, the others including portions of the adjacent States of Massachusetts and Connecticut. The following is a list of the sheets, showing the names assigned to them and their limits in latitude and longitude:

Sheets.	Limits.			
	In latitude.		In longitude.	
	° ′	° ′	° ′	° ′
Franklin	42 00 to	42 15	71 15 to	71 30
Blackstone	42 00	42 15	71 30	71 45
Webster	42 00	42 15	71 45	72 00
Providence	41 45	42 00	71 15	71 30
Burrillville	41 45	42 00	71 30	71 45
Putnam	41 45	42 00	71 45	72 00
Fall River	41 30	41 45	71 00	71 15
Narragansett Bay	41 30	41 45	71 15	71 30
Kent	41 30	41 45	71 30	71 45
Moosup	41 30	41 45	71 45	72 00
Sakonnet	41 15	41 30	71 00	71 15
Newport	41 15	41 30	71 15	71 30
Charlestown	41 15	41 30	71 30	71 45
Stonington	41 15	41 30	71 45	72 00
Block Island	41 00	41 15	71 30	71 45

The spelling of the names conforms to the decisions of the U. S. Board of Geographic Names.

Rhode Island is one of the original thirteen States; it was the last to ratify the Constitution, which it did on May 29, 1790.

The boundary lines between Rhode Island on the one hand and Massachusetts and Connecticut on the other are extremely irregular, having originated with early colonial charters, and having been modified subsequently by conventions and agreements, so that it is impossible to describe them in any other way than by representing them upon a map or by a detailed statement of courses and distances.

The total area of the State is 1,250 square miles. Of this area 197 square miles are water surface, consisting of bays, ponds, rivers, etc., which, deducted from the total area, leaves 1,053 square miles of land surface.

The State is divided into five counties, having land areas as follows:

County.	Square miles.
Bristol	24. 3
Kent	169. 0
Newport	117. 0
Providence	410. 9
Washington	331. 0

These counties are subdivided into towns and cities. There are in the State thirty-four towns and two cities. They are as follows:

Bristol County:
  Barrington.
  Bristol.
  Warren.
Kent County:
  Coventry.
  East Greenwich.
  West Greenwich.
  Warwick.
Newport County:
  Jamestown.
  Little Compton.
  Middletown.
  Newport City.
  New Shoreham.
  Portsmouth.
  Tiverton.
Providence County:
  Burrillville.
  Cranston.
  Cumberland.

Providence County—Continued.
  East Providence.
  Foster.
  Glocester.
  Johnston.
  Lincoln.
  North Providence.
  North Smithfield.
  Pawtucket.
  Providence City.
  Scituate.
  Smithfield.
  Woonsocket.
Washington County:
  Charlestown.
  Exeter.
  Hopkinton.
  North Kingstown.
  South Kingstown.
  Richmond.
  Westerly.

A GEOGRAPHIC DICTIONARY OF RHODE ISLAND.

Names of sheets.

Absalona; hill in Glocester; altitude, 635 feet............... Burrillville.

Adams; fort situated on a point at entrance of Newport Harbor Newport.

Adams; point on shore of Warren River, in Barrington .... Narragansett Bay.

Adamsville; village in southeast part of Little Compton....... Fall River.

Albion; village in Lincoln, on Providence and Worcester R. R . Providence.

Allendale; small village in North Providence.................. Providence.

Allen; harbor on Narragansett Bay, in North Kingstown....... Narragansett Bay.

Allenton; village in North Kingstown........................ Narragansett Bay.

Allenville; village in Smithfield............................. Burrillville.

Almy; point projecting from northern part of Portsmouth into Sakonnet River... Fall River.

Almy; pond in south part of Newport......................... Newport.

Almy; reservoir in Johnston; altitude, 296 feet............... Burrillville.

Andrews; hill on boundary between Warwick and East Greenwich; altitude, 380 feet...................................... Kent.

Anthony; village in Coventry................................ Kent.

Anthony; point projecting from Tiverton into Sakonnet River. Fall River.

Applehouse; hill in Cranston; altitude, 440 feet .... Burrillville.

Apponaug; village and railroad station in Warwick, on New York, Providence and Boston R. R .... Narragansett Bay.

Apponaug; river, or properly an inlet, in Narragansett Bay, in town of Warwick .... Narragansett Bay.

Arcadia; village in northeast part of Richmond .... Kent.

Arctic; village in Warwick.................................. Kent.

Arkwright; village in Coventry .... Kent.

Arnold Mill; village in Cumberland .... Providence.

Arrow; swamp in southeastern part of Exeter................. Kent.

Ashaway; village in southwest part of Hopkinton .... Stonington.

Ashlandville; village in Scituate............................ Burrillville.

Ashton; village in Cumberland.............................. Providence.

Ashville; pond in western part of Hopkinton; height, 169 feet. Moosup.

Auburn; village in Cranston on Providence R. R............... Providence.

Austin Hollow; shallow cove on west shore of Conanicut Island Newport.

Babcock; pond (salt) in south part of Westerly............... Stonington.

Bailey; hill in Richmond; altitude, 240 feet................... Kent.

Baker; village on Warwick R. R., in town of Warwick .... Narragansett Bay.

Bald; hill in West Greenwich; altitude, 630 feet............... Kent.

Bald; hill in Exeter; altitude, 432 feet....................... Kent.

Bald; hill in Warwick; elevation, 220 feet.................... Narragansett Bay.

Bald; hill in Cranston; altitude, 501 feet.................... Burrillville.

Ball; point on east coast of Block Island..................... Block Island.

Bank; village in North Smithfield............................ Burrillville.

Barber; pond in northern part of South Kingstown........... Kent.

Barber Height; hill in southeast part of North Kingston; elevation, 200 feet.. Narragansett Bay.

11

Names of sheets.

Barberville; village in the northeastern part of Hopkinton ..... Kent.

Barden; reservoir in eastern part of Exeter; elevation, 345 feet. Burrillville.

Barrington; river; branch of Warren River in town of Barrington. { Provideuce. Narragansett Bay.

Barrington; town in Bristol County, on shore of Narragansett Bay; area, 9.3 square miles. { Narragansett Bay. Providence.

Barrington; village in northern part of town of same name.... Providence.

Bay Side; village and railroad station on Warwick R. R., in Warwick .... Narragansett Bay.

Beach; pond in Exeter and in eastern Connecticut; elevation, 280 feet .... Moosup.

Beach; pond of salt water near coast of South Kingstown ...... Newport.

Beacon; hill on Block Island; elevation, 200 feet .... Block Island.

Beacon; hill in northern part of Newport; elevation, 120 feet.. Narragansett Bay.

Bear; point projecting into Narragansett Bay from Prudence Island .... Narragansett Bay.

Beaver; river tributary to Pawcatuck River, flowing across Richmond. { Charlestown. Kent.

Beaver Head; point on west shore of Conanicut Island........ Newport.

Beaver Tail; light-house, located at south point of Conanicut Island at entrance to Narragansett Bay...................... Newport.

Bellefonte; village in southeastern part of Cranston........... Providence.

Belleville; pond in eastern part of North Kingstown .... Narragansett Bay.

Belleville; village in North Kingstown........................ Narragansett Bay.

Benedict; pond in southern part of Providence; elevation, 42 feet... Providence.

Bennett; hill in southern part of Foster...................... Burrillville.

Berkeley; village in southern part of Cumberland.............. Providence.

Big; hill in southwestern part of Scituate; altitude, 587 feet .... Burrillville.

Big; river tributary to Pawtuxet River, flowing northward across West Greenwich...................................... Kent.

Biscuit; hill in Foster; altitude, 608 feet .... Kent.

Bishop Rock; island off coast of Newport, in Narragansett Bay. Narragansett Bay.

Bissell; cove entering from Narragansett Bay into North Kingstown .... Narragansett Bay.

Black; point projecting from Portsmouth into Sakonnet River. Fall River.

Black Plain; broad summit in Exeter; altitude, 563 feet....... Kent.

Black Rock; most southerly point of Block Island............ Block Island.

Blackmore; pond in Cranston.................................. Providence.

Blackstone; river heading in Massachusetts and flowing southeast into Seekonk River.................................... Providence.

Bliss Corner; village in Tiverton .... Fall River.

Block; island off south coast of Rhode Island and distant from its nearest point about 10 miles. So named after Adrian Block, its discoverer. It constitutes the town of New Shoreham .... Block Island.

Blue; pond in eastern part of Hopkinton; elevation, 235 feet... Kent.

Blue; pond in western part of Hopkinton; height, 235 feet..... Moosup.

Blue Bill; cove from Sakonnet River, in northern part of Portsmouth... Fall River.

Bonnet; point on east coast of South Kingstown.............. Newport.

Bonnet, The; hill on east coast of South Kingstown........... Newport.

Boon; pond in Exeter; elevation, 347 feet .... Kent.

Borden; brook, tributary to Sakonnet River, in Tiverton....... Fall River.

Boston; hill in eastern part of Coventry; altitude, 320 feet..... Kent.

Names of sheets.

Boston Neck; projection of land between the main coast and The Cove, in South Kingstown .... Newport.

Bowdish; reservoir in eastern part of Glocester; height, 550 feet .... Putnam.

Bowen; hill in Coventry; height, 610 feet...................... Kent.

Bradley; hill in Providence; altitude, 190 feet................. Providence.

Branch; river in Burrillville, tributary to the Blackstone River. Burrillville.

Brandy; brook in Glocester .... Burrillville.

Breakheart; hill in southern part of West Greenwich; altitude 340 feet.. Kent.

Brenton; cove on west coast of Newport....................... Newport.

Brenton; point on south coast of Newport..................... Newport.

Brenton Reef; submerged rock at entrance to Narragansett Bay, over which is anchored a light vessel.................. Newport.

Bridgetown; village in South Kingstown...................... Newport.

Bristol; harbor of the village of the same name, being an inlet from Narragansett Bay...................................... Narragansett Bay.

Bristol; town of Bristol County on the shore of Narragansett Bay; area, 9.1 square miles. { Narragansett Bay. Fall River.

Bristol; the principal village in the town of Bristol, on Bristol Harbor, reached by the Providence, Warren and Bristol R. R. Narragansett Bay.

Bristol Neck; promontory projecting between Narragansett and Mount Hope Bays, and constituting the town of Bristol and part of the town of Warren. } Fall River. Narragansett Bay.

Broad; hill in southern part of South Kingstown; altitude, 226 feet.. Charlestown.

Brown; point projecting from Tiverton into Sakonnet River ... Fall River.

Brush Neck; peninsula extending into Narragansett Bay from town of Warwick... Narragansett Bay.

Brushy; brook tributary to Pawcatuck River, in Hopkinton... Kent.

Buck; hill in western part of Burrillville; height, 728 feet..... Putnam.

Buckhorn; brook tributary to Moosup River, in Coventry... Kent.

Buckeye; brook, the outlet of Warwick Pond, draining it into Narragansett Bay, in Warwick............................ Narragansett Bay.

Bullock; point in town of Barrington, Bristol County, projecting into Narragansett Bay...................................... Narragansett Bay.

Bullock Neck; peninsula projecting into Narragansett Bay from town of East Providence............................... Providence.

Bull; point on east coast of Conanicut Island, projecting into Narragansett Bay.. Newport.

Burdickville; village in Hopkinton .... Charlestown.

Burgess; cove, a slight indentation from Providence River, in southern part of Providence.............................. Providence.

Burlingame; reservoir in Glocester; elevation, 590 feet ...... Burrillville.

Burnt; hill in Scituate; altitude, 424 feet..................... Kent.

Burrillville; town in northwestern part of Providence County; area 53·2 square miles. { Blackstone. Putnam. Burrillville.

Burrillville; village in town of Burrillville .... Burrillville.

Buttonwood; village and railroad station on the Warwick R. R., in Warwick.. Narragansett Bay.

Butts; hill in Portsmouth; elevation, 180 feet................. { Fall River. Narragansett Bay.

Calf Neck; projection from town of North Kingstown into Mill Cove .... Narragansett Bay.

Names of sheets.

Canob; pond in western part of Richmond .... Kent.
Canopaug; brook tributary to Pawtuxet River................ Burrillville.
Carbuncle; hill in northwestern part of Coventry; altitude, 513 feet... Moosup.
Carbuncle; pond in the western part of Coventry; elevation, 355 feet... Moosup.
Card; ponds (salt) on the coast of South Kingstown........... Charlestown.
Carolina; village in Richmond................................... Charlestown.
Carr; point on coast of Portsmouth, projecting into Narragansett Bay... Narragansett Bay.
Carr; pond in eastern part of West Greenwich; elevation, 327 feet .... Kent.
Casey; hill in Exeter; altitude, 442 feet........................ Kent.
Casey; point projecting from North Kingstown into Narragansett Bay... Narragansett Bay.
Castle; hill on coast of Newport................................ Newport.
Cat Rocks; hill in Johnston; elevation, 360 feet .... Burrillville.
Catamint; small brook tributary to Blackstone River, in Cumberland... Providence.
Cedar Swamp; brook tributary to Pawtuxet river, in Johnston... Burrillville.
Cedar Swamp; brook tributary to Charles River, in Charlestown... Charlestown.
Cedar Swamp; pond in southern part of South Kingstown .... Charlestown.
Cedar Swamp; pond in western part of Burrillville........... Putnam.
Center; village on Block Island .... Block Island.
Centerdale; village in North Providence, on Providence and Springfield R. R .... Providence.
Centerville; village in Hopkinton............................... Kent.
Centerville; village in Warwick .... Kent.
Central Falls; village in Lincoln................................ Providence.
Chagum; pond of salt water in southern part of Block Island.. Block Island.
Champlain; hill in western part of Hopkinton; elevation, 400 feet ... . Stonington.
Charles; river, a large branch of Pawcatuck River, forming boundary between Charlestown and Richmond............. Charlestown.
Charlestown; sand beach on south coast of Charlestown ...... Charlestown.
Charlestown; inlet through Charlestown Beach into Minigret Pond .... Charlestown.
Charlestown; town in southern part of Washington County; area, 39·8 square miles... Charlestown.
Charlestown; village in Charlestown .... Charlestown.
Chase; cove entering from Kickamuit River into southern part of town of Warwick... Fall River.
Chepachet; river in Burrillville and Glocester .... Burrillville.
Chepachet; village in Glocester .... Burrillville.
Cherry; brook tributary to Blackstone River, in North Smithfield... Burrillville.
Chipuxet; river tributary to Charles River, in South Kingstown Charlestown.
Chopmist; hill in northwestern part of Scituate; altitude, 730 feet .... Burrillville.
Chopmist; village in Scituate.................................... Burrillville.
Church; cove indenting coast of Little Compton .... Sakonnet.
Church; cove from Mount Hope Bay extending into Bristol Neck Fall River.

Names of sheets.

Church; point projecting from Tiverton into Sakonnet River... Fall River.

Church; point projecting from coast of Little Compton into Sakonnet River .... Sakonnet.

Clapman; pond in Westerly...................................... Stonington.

Clark; point projecting from North Kingstown into Narragansett Bay .... Narragansett Bay.

Clay Head; cliff on east coast of Block Island .... Block Island.

Clayville; village in Scituate.................................. Burrillville.

Clyde; village in Warwick, on Pawtuxet River.................. Kent.

Coasters Harbor; island off coast of Newport, in Narragansett Bay .... Narragansett Bay.

Coddington; cove, an arm of Narragansett Bay, extending into Middletown .... Narragansett Bay.

Coggeshall; cove, part of Narragansett Bay, projecting into Prudence Island .... Narragansett Bay.

Coggeshall; point on coast of Portsmouth, projecting into Narragansett Bay .... Narragansett Bay.

Coles; village and railroad station on the Warwick R. R., in Warwick .... Narragansett Bay.

Colvin; brook, branch of Pawtuxet River, in Scituate.......... Kent.

Common Fence; southernmost point of Rhode Island .... Fall River.

Conanicut; island in southern part of Narragansett Bay, comprising the town of Jamestown, Newport County............ Newport.

Congdon; hill in southern part of North Kingstown; elevation, 220 feet... Narragansett Bay.

Conimicut; point projecting into Narragansett Bay from town of Warwick... Narragansett Bay.

Conimicut; village and railroad station on Warwick R. R. in Warwick .... Narragansett Bay.

Cooke Store; village in northwest part of Foster.............. Putnam.

Copper Mine; hill in Cumberland; altitude 400 feet........... Providence.

Cork; brook tributary to Pawtuxet River .... Burrillville.

Corliss; cove from Providence River, in southern portion of Providence.. Providence.

Cormorant; pond, part of Great Salt Pond, on Block Island.... Block Island.

Cormorant Rock; island off coast of Middletown.............. Sakonnet.

Cornelius; island off north coast of Kingstown, in Narragansett Bay... Narragansett Bay.

Cove, The; indentation from Sakonnet River, in southern part of Portsmouth.. Fall River.

Cove, The; body of salt water in town of South Kingstown ... Newport.

Coventry; town in Kent County, area 17·1 square miles....... { Kent.
{ Moosup.

Coventry Center; village in Coventry .... Kent.

Cow; cove indenting northern part of Block Island .... Block Island.

Coweset; village and railroad station upon New York, Providence & Boston R. R., in town of Warwick................ Narragansett Bay.

Cranston; town in Providence County, area 30·2 square miles. { Narragansett Bay.
{ Providence.
{ Burrillville.
{ Kent.

Cranston; village in northern part of Cranston............... Providence.

Cranston Print Works; village in northern part of Cranston.. Providence.

Names of sheets.

Crescent; beach on east coast of Block Island .... Block Island.
Crompton; village in Warwick...................................... Kent.
Crookfall; brook tributary to Blackstone River,in Lincoln...... Providence.
Cumberland; hill in Cumberland; altitude, 342 feet............ Providence.
Cumberland; town in Providence County; area, 27·5 square
    miles .... Franklin.
Cumberland; village in Cumberland, on Blackstone River..... Providence.
Cumberland Mills; village in southern part of Cumberland... Providence.
Cunliff; pond in eastern part of Cranston...................... Providence.
Davisville; village in North Kingstown .... Narragansett Bay.
Dead; swamp in southeastern part of West Greenwich......... Kent.
Deep; pond in southwest part of Exeter; elevation, 310 feet... Moosup.
Diamond; hill in southwest part of Hopkinton; elevation, 220
    feet.. Stonington.
Diamond Hill; village in Cumberland.......................... Providence.
Dickens; most westerly point of Block Island.................. Block Island.
Drownville; village in Barrington .... Narragansett Bay.
Drum Rock; hill in Warwick, Kent County; elevation, 220 feet. Narragansett Bay.
Dry; brook tributary to Pawtuxet River, in Johnston........... Burrillville.
Duck; pond in town of Warwick................................ Narragansett Bay.
Dumping Rock; hill in eastern part of Exeter; altitude, 242
    feet .... Kent.
Dumplings; group of rocks off east coast of Conanicut Island,
    in Narragansett Bay .... Newport.
Dunnell Print Works; village in Pawtucket.................... Providence.
Durfee; hill in Glocester; elevation, 805 feet; highest eleva-
    tion in the State... Burrillville.
Dutch; island in Narragansett Bay .... Narragansett Bay.
Dutch Island; harbor, arm of Narragansett Bay, projecting ⎰ Newport.
    into Conanicut Island.   ⎱ Narragansett Bay.
Dye; hill in Exeter and Hopkinton; altitude, 469 feet.......... Moosup.
Dyer; island in Narragansett Bay, off coast of Portsmouth, of
    which town it forms a part................................ Narragansett Bay.
Dyerville; village in Johnston, on Providence and Springfield
    R. R.. Providence.
East; island off coast of Little Compton...................... Sakonnet.
East Greenwich; town in Kent County; area, 17·1 square ⎰ Kent.
    miles.   ⎱ Narragansett Bay.
East Greenwich; principal village in town of same name...... Narragansett Bay.
Easton; beach on coast of Middletown .... Newport.
Easton; point on coast of Middletown......................... Newport.
Easton; salt-water pond on coast between Newport and Middle-
    town .... Newport.
East Providence; town in Providence County; area, 12·5 square
    miles .... Providence.
East Providence; principal village in town of same name ..... Providence.
East Providence Center; village in northern part of East Prov-
    idence.. Providence.
Edgewood; village in eastern part of Cranston................ Providence.
Eldridge; creek flowing into Narragansett Bay from North
    Kingstown .... Narragansett Bay.
Ell; pond in western part of Hopkinton .... Moosup.
Elmdale; village in Scituate .... Burrillville.

Names of sheets.

Escoheag; hill in southwestern part of Greenwich; altitude, 541 feet.. Moosup.

Escoheag; village in western part of Greenwich............... Moosup.

Exeter; town in northern part of Washington County; area, 58 square miles. { Kent. Moosup.

Exeter Hill; village in eastern part of Exeter................. Kent.

Fenner; hill in eastern part of Hopkinton; altitude, 367 feet .. Kent.

Fenner; pond in eastern part of Cranston..................... Providence.

Field; hill in southwestern part of Scituate; altitude, 573 feet. Burrillville.

Field; point projecting into Providence river at its mouth from southern part of town of Providence....................... Providence.

Fish; cove on coast of South Kingstown....................... Charlestown.

Fisher; hill in northern part of West Greenwich; altitude, 471 feet .... Kent.

Fishing; cove from Narragansett Bay into North Kingstown.... Narragansett Bay.

Fiskville; village in Cranston.................................. Kent.

Flat; river tributary to Wood River in, West Greenwich....... Kent.

Flat; river tributary to Pawtuxet River, in Coventry.......... Kent.

Flat River; reservoir in Coventry; elevation, 249 feet.......... Kent.

Flint; point on coast of Middletown, extending into Sakonnet River... Sakonnet.

Fogland; point projecting from Tiverton into Sakonnet River.. Fall River.

Fones; pond in eastern part of Coventry....................... Kent.

Forestdale; village in North Smithfield........................ Burrillville.

Fort; hill rising from Providence River to an altitude of 80 feet. Providence.

Foster; town in southern part of Providence County; area, 48·8 square miles. { Kent. Burrillville. Putnam. Moosup.

Foster; village in northwest part of Foster.................... Putnam.

Foster Center; village in Foster .... Burrillville.

Foster Ledge; hill in Coventry; elevation, 508 feet............ Kent.

Fountain Spring; village in Johnston.......................... Burrillville.

Fox; hill in Bristol... Narragansett Bay.

Fox; island off coast of North Kingstown, in Narragansett Bay.. Narragansett Bay.

Fox; point projecting from Providence into Providence River at mouth of Seekonk River................................. Providence.

Freebody; hill on Conanicut Island........................... Narragansett Bay.

Frenchtown; village in East Greenwich....................... Kent.

Fresh; pond on Block Island .... Block Island.

Fruit; hill in North Providence; altitude, 240 feet .... Providence.

Fuller; rock at mouth of Providence River near middle of channel Providence.

Gardiner; pond of salt water in south part of Middletown..... Newport.

Gaspee; point projecting into Narragansett Bay from town of Warwick... Narragansett Bay.

Gates; pond in Richmond...................................... Kent.

Gazzaville; village in Burrillville .... Burrillville.

Geneva; village in North Providence.......................... Providence.

Georgiaville; pond in Smithfield; elevation, 557 feet .... Burrillville.

Georgiaville; village in Smithfield .... Burrillville.

Glendale; village in Burrillville .... Burrillville.

Glen Rock; village in South Kingstown........................ Kent.

Globe Village; village in Woonsocket......................... Burrillville.

Names of sheets.

Glocester; town in northwestern part of Providence County; { Burrillville. / Putnam. } area, 53·2 square miles.

Goat; low, sandy island at entrance to Newport Harbor........ Newport.

Gooseberry; island off the coast of Newport.................. Newport.

Gorton; pond in town of Warwick........................... Narragansett Bay.

Gould; island in Sakonnet River........................... Fall River.

Gould; island in Narragansett Bay......................... Narragansett Bay.

Grace; cove in west coast of Block Island................... Block Island.

Grace; point on west coast of Block Island................. Block Island.

Graniteville; village in Johnston on Providence and Springfield R. R... Providence.

Graniteville; village in Burrillville...................... Burrillville.

Grass; pond in southern part of Coventry; altitude, 432 feet... Kent.

Grassy; pond in western part of Hopkinton; height, 362 feet.. Moosup.

Graves; point on coast of Newport.......................... Newport.

Great; swamp in South Kingstown and Richmond, bordering upon Worden Pond... Charlestown.

Great Salt; pond of salt water upon Block Island........... Block Island.

Green; hill near south coast of South Kingstown; elevation, 60 feet... Charlestown.

Green; island in Narragansett Bay, off coast of town of Warwick .... Narragansett Bay.

Greene; point projecting from North Kingstown into Narragansett Bay... Narragansett Bay.

Greene; village in Coventry............................... Kent.

Green Hill; pond of salt water on coast of South Kingstown... Charlestown.

Greenville; village in Smithfield......................... Burrillville.

Greenwich; bay, part of Narragansett Bay in towns of East Greenwich and Warwick................................... Narragansett Bay.

Greenwich; cove of Greenwich Bay, projecting inland between East Greenwich and Warwick.............................. Narragansett Bay.

Greenwood; village and railroad station upon New York, Providence and Boston R. R., in town of Warwick............. Narragansett Bay.

Greystone; village in North Providence.................... Providence.

Grove; point on east coast of Block Island................ Block Island.

Gull; point projecting into Narragansett Bay from Prudence Island .... Narragansett Bay.

Gull Rocks; rocky islands in Narragansett Bay off coast of Newport... Narragansett Bay.

Halfway Rock; island off coast of Little Compton........... Sakonnet.

Hall; creek flowing into Narragansett Bay from North Kingstown .... Narragansett Bay.

Hamilton; hill in southern part of North Kingstown; elevation, 220 feet.. Narragansett Bay.

Hamilton; village on coast of North Kingstown............. Narragansett Bay.

Hammond; pond in Pawtucket............................... Providence.

Hannah; brook tributary to Pawtuxet River in Glocester and Scituate .... Burrillville.

Harbor; pond of salt water upon Block Island.............. Block Island.

Harbor, The; village on east coast of Block Island .... Block Island.

Harkney; hill in Coventry; elevation, 506 feet............. Kent.

Harmony; village in Glocester............................ Burrillville.

Harris; village in northern part of Coventry on Pawtuxet River. Kent.

Harrisdale; village in Scituate........................... Burrillville.

Names of sheets.

Harrisville; village in Burrillville............................ Burrillville.
Hemlock; brook tributary to Pawtuxet River................. Burrillville.
Hen; island in Sakonnet River .... Fall River.
Herring; pond in Burrillville; elevation, 392 feet............. Burrillville.
High Hill; point projecting from Tiverton into Sakonnet River. Fall River.
Hillsdale; village in Richmond................................ Kent.
Hills Grove; village and railroad station upon New York, Providence and Boston R. R. in town of Warwick................. Narragansett Bay.
Hog; island in Narragansett Bay, off coast of Bristol.......... Narragansett Bay.
Hope, Mount; hill on southern part of Bristol Neck in town of Bristol; altitude, 200 feet.................................... Fall River.
Hope; village in Cranston...................................... Kent.
Hope Valley; village in Hopkinton .... Kent.
Hopkins; hill in eastern part of West Greenwich; elevation, 487 feet.. Kent.
Hopkins; pond in northern part of Exeter; elevation, 337 feet. Kent.
Hopkins Hollow; village in western part of Coventry.......... Moosup.
Hopkins Mills; village in Foster .... Burrillville.

Hopkinton; town in the southwest part of Washington County; area, 43·6 square miles. ⎰ Stonington. / Moosup. / Charlestown. / Kent.

Hopkinton; village in town of same name .... Stonington.
Horse Neck; peninsula extending into Narragansett Bay from town of Warwick... Narragansett Bay.
Howard; hill in southern part of Foster; altitude, 687 feet .... Burrillville.
Hoxie; village and railroad station on Warwick R. R., in Warwick .... Narragansett Bay.
Huckleberry; hill in western part of North Kingstown; altitude, 250 feet.. Kent.
Hughesdale; village in southern part of Johnston.............. Providence.
Hull; cove in east coast of Conanicut Island, Narragansett Bay.. Newport.
Hummock; point projecting from northern part of Portsmouth into Sakonnet River .... Fall River.
Hungry; hill in northern part of West Greenwich; elevation, 405 feet.. Kent.
Hunting; hill in Cumberland; altitude, 400 feet .... Providence.
Hunting House; brook tributary to Pawtuxet River, in Glocester and Scituate .... Burrillville.
Huntsville; village in Burrillville............................ Burrillville.
Hygeia Mount; hill in northwest part of Foster; height, 700 feet... Putnam.
India; point projecting from East Providence into Seekonk River... Providence.
Indian; river flowing into Saugatucket River, in South Kingstown .... Newport
Indian Cedar; swamp in northern part of Charlestown........ Charlestown.
Island Rocks; group of small islands at mouth of Sakonnet River... Sakonnet.
Jackson; village in Cranston .... Kent.
Jacob; point on shore of Warren River, in Barrington .... Narragansett Bay.
James; pond in Exeter; elevation, 354 feet .... Kent.
Jamestown; town of Newport County, comprising Conanicut Island; area, 9·5 square miles............................... Newport.

Names of sheets.

Jenks; hill in Lincoln; altitude, 400 feet .... Providence.
Jerimoth; hill in northwest part of Foster; height, 799 feet ... Putnam.
Johnston; town in Providence County; area 24·1 square { Burrillville.
miles.   { Providence.
Judith; point, the southernmost extremity of town of South
Kingstown, at entrance of Narragansett Bay................. Newport.
Keech; pond in Glocester; elevation 438 feet.................... Burrillville.
Kent; brook tributary to Pawtuxet river....................... Burrillville.
Kent; village in Scituate..................................... Burrillville.
Kenyon; hill in Richmond; altitude 272 feet .... Charlestown.
Kenyon; village in Richmond.................................. Charleston.
Kettle; point projecting into Providence River from town of
East Providence .... Providence.
Kickamuit; river heading in Warren Reservoir, Massachu- ⎧ Fall River.
setts, and flowing through town of Warren into Mount ⎨ Narragansett Bay.
Hope Bay.   ⎩
Killy; brook tributary to Pawtuxet river in Glocester and Scit-
uate... Burrillville.
Killingly; pond in southwest corner of Glocester and in eastern
part of Connecticut.. Putnam.
Kingstown; hill in South Kingstown; altitude 252 feet........ Charlestown.
Kingstown; village in South Kingstown .... Charlestown.
Knightsville; village in Cranston, on New York and New Eng-
land R. R... Providence.
Lafayette; village in North Kingstown .... Narragansett Bay.
Larkin; pond in South Kingstown............................. Charlestown
Laurel Hill; hill in Cranston; altitude, 460 feet............... Burrillville.
Lawton; hill in Cranston; altitude, 460 feet .... Burrillville.
Lawton Valley; village in Portsmouth, on coast of Narragan-
sett Bay and on Old Colony and Newport R. R.............. Narragansett Bay.
Leonard; pond in Providence . ... Providence.
Leonards Corner; small village in East Providence............ Providence.
Lily; pond in south part of Newport .... Newport.
Lime Rock; island in Newport Harbor, on which a light-house
is established... Newport.
Lime Rock; village in Lincoln................................ Providence.
Lincoln; town in Providence County; area 19·7 square miles... Providence.
Lippitt; village in Warwick on Pawtuxet River .... Kent.
Little; pond in Cumberland.................................. Providence.
Little; river in North Smithfield .... Burrillville.
Little Compton; town in southeastern part of Newport county; { Sakonnet.
area 21·4 square miles.   { Fall River.
Little Compton; village in Little Compton .... Fall River.
Little Grass; pond in southeastern part of Coventry........... Kent.
Little Narragansett; bay at mouth of Pawcatuck River, partly
in Rhode Island and partly in Connecticut .... Stonington.
Little Neck; pond of salt water near coast of South Kingstown. Newport.
Little Neck; projection of land between the coast and The
Cove in South Kingstown................................... Newport.
Little Neck; projection from southern part of town of Warren
into Kickamuit river .... Fall River.
Little Sand; pond in town of Warwick........................ Narragansett Bay.
Little Tree; point projecting from North Kingstown, into Nar-
ragansett Bay.. Narragansett Bay.

GANNETT.] A GEOGRAPHIC DICTIONARY OF RHODE ISLAND. 21

Names of sheets.

Locustville; pond in eastern part of Hopkinton .... Kent.
Locustville; village in eastern part of Hopkinton .... Kent.
Lone; pond in southern part of South Kingstown .... Charlestown.
Long; point on south of Greenwich Bay, in town of Warwick.. Narragansett Bay.
Long; pond in western part of Hopkinton..................... Moosup.
Long; pond in southern part of Providence; elevation, 56 feet.. Providence.
Long Neck; cove from Sakonnet River in northern part of
    Portsmouth... Fall River.
Lonsdale; village in southeastern part of Lincoln .... Providence.
Lonsdale Station; village in southern part of Cumberland .... Providence.
Lorraine Mills; village in Pawtucket .... Providence.
Lottery; small village in Westerly, near mouth Pawtucket
    River... Stonington.
Lymanville; village in North Providence .... Providence.
Mackerel; cove from Narragansett Bay into Conanicut Island,
    cutting it nearly asunder.................................. Newport.
Manton; village in Providence .... Providence.
Manville; village in northern part of Lincoln................. Providence.
Mapleville; village in Burrillville.......................... Burrillville.
Marsh; island in upper part of Narragansett Bay.............. Providence.
Marsh; point on south of Greenwich Bay, in town of Warwick.. Narragansett Bay.
Mashapaug; pond in southern part of Providence; elevation, 40
    feet.. Providence.
Matoonoc; village on coast of South Kingstown .... Charlestown.
McCurry; point projecting from Portsmouth into Sakonnet River Fall River.
McSparran; hill in South Kingstown; elevation, 236 feet ...... Newport.
Meadow; brook tributary to Charles River, in Richmond ...... Charlestown.
Merino; village in Johnston on Providence and Springfield R. R. Providence.
Miantonomy; hill in northern part of Newport; elevation, 120
    feet.. Narragansett Bay.
Middle; pond of salt water in southern part of Block Island.... Block Island.
Middletown; town in southern part of Newport County; area, { Fall River. Narragansett Bay. Sakonnet. Newport.
    12·5 square miles.
Mill; cove from Narragansett Bay into North Kingstown....... Narragansett Bay.
Miller; river tributary to Blackstone River, in Cumberland ... Providence.
Millgut; pond of salt water in Popasquash Neck, Bristol........ Narragansett Bay.
Millville; village in Exeter................................. Kent.
Mink; brook tributary to Worden Pond, in South Kingstown.. Charlestown.
Misery, Mount; hill in Scituate; altitude, 510 feet............ Kent.
Mishnock; pond in northern part of West Greenwich; elevation,
    250 feet .... Kent.
Mishnock; river tributary to Pawtuxet River, in Coventry..... Kent.
Mishnock; swamp in southern part of Coventry................ Kent.
Mohegan; village in Burrillville .... Burrillville.
Mooresfield; village in South Kingstown .... Newport.
Moosup; river tributary to Quinebaug River .... Putnam.
Moosup Valley; village in southwest part of Foster........... Moosup.
Morgan Mills; village in southern part of Johnston........... Providence.
Moscow; village in Hopkinton............................... Kent.
Moshassuck; river tributary to Blackstone River, in Lincoln.. Providence.
Mosquitohawk; brook tributary to Pawtuxet River, in Glo-
    cester and Scituate .... Burrillville.
Moswansicut; pond in Scituate; altitude, 300 feet.............

Names of sheets.

Moswansicut; river tributary to Pawtuxet River .... Burrillville.

Mount Hope; bay, easterly arm of Narragansett Bay.......... Fall River.

Mount Hope; southern point of Bristol .... Fall River.

Mountain Dale; village in Smithfield......................... Burrillville.

Muscle Shoal; reef off coast of Portsmouth, in Narragansett
Bay .... Narragansett Bay.

Nag; pond of salt water in Prudence Island, town of Portsmouth.. Narragansett Bay.

Nannaquacket; pond of salt-water in western part of Tiverton. Fall River.

Nannasatucket; river, outlet of Belleville Pond, emptying into
Narragansett Bay, in North Kingstown...................... Narragansett Bay.

Napatree; beach forming south boundary of Little Narragansett Bay, in Westerly .... Stonington.

Napatree; point on sandy beach of same name, in Westerly .... Stonington.

Narragansett Bay; arm of sea projecting into interior of ⎰Narragansett Bay.
Rhode Island. It contains numerous large islands and ⎱Providence.
affords many excellent harbors.   ⎰Newport.

Narragansett Pier; summer resort upon east coast, South Kingstown .... Newport.

Narrows, the; contracted mouth of Kickamuit River.......... Fall River.

Nasonville; village in Burrillville............................ Burrillville.

Neck, the; subdivision of city of Newport..................... Newport.

Neutaconkanut; hill in southern part of Johnston; altitude,
280 feet.. Providence.

Newport; city constituting south part of Rhode Island, in
south part Newport County; area, 7·9 square miles.......... Newport.

New Shoreham; town in Newport County, comprising Block
Island; area 10·5 square miles.............................. Block Island.

New York and New England; railroad running southwest from
Boston through Rhode Island and Connecticut, with numerous branches.

New York, Providence and Boston; railroad, whose main line
connects New Haven, Conn., with Providence, R. I., and
Boston, Mass.; has many branches, principally in southeast
Massachusetts.

Niantic; village in Westerly.................................... Charlestown.

Ninigret; pond (salt) separated from the sea by Charlestown
beach .... Charlestown.

Nipmuc; hill in Scituate; altitude, 561 feet.................... Kent.

No Bottom; pond in Richmond................................. Kent.

Nonquit; pond (salt) in southwest part of Tiverton............ Fall River.

Noose Neck; village in West Greenwich .... Kent.

Noose Neck; hill in southern part of West Greenwich; altitude,
511 feet.. Kent.

North; point projecting into Narragansett Bay from town of
Bristol .... Narragansett Bay.

North; point projecting into Narragansett Bay from Prudence
Island .... Narragansett Bay.

North; point on coast of Conanicut Island..................... Narragansett Bay.

North Kingstown; town in Washington County bordering on ⎰Kent.
Narragansett Bay; area, 42·6 square miles.   ⎱Narragansett Bay.

North Providence; town in Providence County; area, 5·5 square
miles .... Providence.

North Scituate; village in Scituate............................ Burrillville.

Names of sheets.

North Smithfield; town in Providence County; area, 24·2 square miles. ⎱ Blackstone. Burrillville. Providence.

Northwest; point projecting into Narragansett Bay from Patience Island .... Narragansett Bay.

Norwood; village and railway station in Warwick............. Providence.

Noyes Beach; village on coast of Westerly.................... Stonington.

Noyes; point on coast of Westerly............................. Stonington.

Oak Valley; village in Burrillville .... Burrillville.

Oak Swamp; reservoir in Johnston; altitude, 364 feet......... Burrillville.

Oakland; village in Burrillville................................ Burrillville.

Oakland Beach; village and railroad station on Warwick R. R., in Warwick .... Narragansett Bay.

Ochre; point on coast of Newport............................. Newport.

Occupasspatuxet; cove from Narragansett Bay, in town of Warwick... .... Narragansett Bay.

Old Colony and Newport; branch of Old Colony Railroad running southward to Newport.

Old Harbor; point on east coast of Block Island .... Block Island.

Old Mill; an inlet, called a creek, from Narragansett Bay, in town of Warwick.. Narragansett Bay.

Old Orchard; cove from Sakonnet River, in northern part of Portsmouth.. Fall River.

Old Warwick; cove in Narragansett Bay in town of Warwick Narragansett Bay.

Olney; pond in Lincoln.. Providence.

Olneyville; village in Johnston, on Providence and Springfield R. R.. Providence.

Omega; village in northern part of East Providence.......... Providence.

One Hundred Acre; cove of Barrington River, in town of Barrington... Providence.

One Hundred Acre; pond in South Kingstown .... ⎱ Charlestown. Kent.

Pachet; brook, tributary to Sakonnet River, in town of Little Compton .... Fall River.

Paine; brook, tributary to Pawtuxet River, in Foster........... Burrillville.

Paradise Rock; hill in southern part of Middletown .... Newport.

Parris; brook, tributary to Pawcatuck River, in Exeter........ Moosup.

Pascoag; reservoir in Burrillville; elevation, 451 feet.......... Burrillville.

Pascoag; village in Burrillville................................ Burrillville.

Pasquiset; pond in northeastern part of Charlestown; elevation, 92 feet.. Charlestown.

Passeonkquis; pond (salt), an inlet from Narragansett Bay, in town of Warwick .... Narragansett Bay.

Patience; island in Narragansett Bay; part of town in Portsmouth.. Narragansett Bay.

Pattaquamscott; river in South Kingstown................... Newport.

Pawcatuck; river of considerable importance, heading in southwest part of the State and forming boundary between many of the towns, and, in its lower course, boundary line between Rhode Island and Connecticut. Empties into Little Narragansett Bay. ⎱ Charlestown. Stonington.

Pawtucket; town in Providence County; area, 8·5 square miles. Providence.

Pawtuxet; river tributary to Narragansett Bay, forming boundary between Cranston and Warwick .... Providence.

Names of sheets.

Pawtuxet; village in eastern part of Cranston............... Providence.

Pawtuxet; river flowing through central part of State and emptying into head of Narragansett Bay.   { Narragansett Bay. Burrillville. Kent.

Pawtuxet Station; village and railway station in northeast part of Warwick .... Providence.

Peacedale; village in South Kingstown .... Newport.

Penny; hill in southern part of West Greenwich; altitude, 338 feet .... Kent.

Perryville; village in South Kingstown........................ Charlestown.

Pilot; hill on Block Island .... Block Island.

Pine; hill in Johnston; altitude, 529 feet .... Burrillville.

Pine; hill in Exeter; elevation, 543 feet........................ Kent.

Pine; hill in Richmond; altitude, 329 feet .... Kent.

Pine Hill; point projecting into Narragansett Bay from Providence Island... Narragansett Bay.

Pine Hill; broad strip of elevated land in southwest part of Glocester... Putnam.

Pine Swamp; reservoir in eastern part of Scituate; elevation, 391 feet... Burrillville.

Phenix; village in Warwick and on Pawtuxet River .... Kent.

Plainville; village in Burrillville............................... Burrillville.

Plainville; village in Richmond .... Charlestown.

Pleasant Mount; hill in northern part of South Kingstown; height, 383 feet... Kent.

Pocasset; hill in Tiverton; altitude, 340 feet.................. Fall River.

Pocasset; river, a branch of Pawtuxet River, flowing through Johnston.   { Burrillville. Providence.

Pocasset; railway station in Warwick .... Providence.

Poquiant; brook tributary to Pawcatuck River, draining Watchaug Pond... Charlestown.

Point Judith; pond (salt) on coast of South Kingstown........ Charlestown.

Point Judith Neck; southern part of town of South Kingstown, lying between the open sea and Point Judith Pond .... Newport.

Pomham Rock; island in Narragansett Bay near its head ..... Providence.

Ponaganset; reservoir in Glocester; elevation, 635 feet........ Burrillville

Ponaganset; river tributary to Pawtuxet River................ Burrillville.

Ponaganset; village in Scituate................................ Burrillville.

Pontiac; village in Warwick on Pawtuxet Valley R. R .... Narragansett Bay.

Popasquash; point, the southern extremity of Popasquash Neck, in town of Bristol... Narragansett Bay.

Popasquash Neck; peninsula projecting into Narragansett Bay, forming part of town of Bristol...................... Narragansett Bay.

Poplar; point projecting from North Kingstown into Narragansett Bay .... Narragansett Bay.

Portsmouth; town in Newport County bordering on Narragansett Bay; area, 23·4 square miles.   { Narragansett Bay. Fall River.

Portsmouth; village in Portsmouth .... Fall River.

Portsmouth Grove; village in Portsmouth on coast of Narragansett Bay and on Old Colony and Newport R. R .... Narragansett Bay.

Potowomut; river draining into Narragansett Bay and forming part of boundary between East Greenwich, North Kingstown and Warwick .... Narragansett Bay.

Names of sheets.

Potowomut Neck; peninsula, part of Warwick, which projects into Greenwich Bay and Potowomut River.................. Narragansett Bay.

Potter; cove, a part of Narragansett Bay entering Prudence Island.. Narragansett Bay.

Potter; cove, entering Conanicut Island from Narragansett Bay. Narragansett Bay.

Potter Hill; village in southwest part of Hopkinton.......... Stonington.

Potterville; village in Coventry .... Kent.

Pray; hill on line between Glocester and Foster; elevation, 693 feet... Burrillville.

Premisy; hill in North Smithfield; altitude, 340 feet........... Burrillville.

Primrose Station; village and railway station in North Smithfield .... Burrillville.

Print Works; pond in northern part of Cranston............... Providence.

Providence; city in Providence County; the largest and most important in the State; area, 15·7 square miles.............. Providence.

Prudence; island in Narragansett Bay, forming part of town of Portsmouth... Narragansett Bay·

Quaker; hill in Portsmouth; elevation, 260 feet................ Narragansett Bay.

Queens; river tributary to Powcatuck River, flowing southwesterly through Exeter.................................... Kent.

Quicksand; pond (salt) near coast in town of Little Compton.. Fall River.

Quidnick; reservoir in Coventry; altitude, 476 feet........... Kent.

Quidnick; village in Coventry................................. Kent.

Quonset; point projecting from North Kingstown.

Quonochontaug; pond (salt) separated from the sea by Quonochontaug Beach .... Charlestown.

Quonochontaug; village in Westerly........................... Charlestown.

Quonochontaug Beach; sand bar on coast of Charlestown.... Charlestown.

Rabbit; island off coast of North Kingstown, in Narragansett Bay .... Narragansett Bay.

Raccoon; hill in West Greenwich; altitude, 601 feet........... Kent.

Randall; pond in northern part of Cranston................... Providence.

Rhode Island, also called Aquidneck; large island in Narragansett Bay, comprising towns of Newport, Middletown, and Portsmouth.. Newport.

Rice; village in western part of Coventry..................... Moosup.

Richmond; town in southern part of Washington county; { Charlestown. area, 38·9 square miles. { Kent.

Richmond; village in Scituate .... Burrillville.

Richmond Paper Company; village in northern part of East Providence .... Providence.

River View; village and railway station on Warwick R. R., in Warwick .... Narragansett Bay.

Riverpoint; in Warwick, on Pawtuxet River.................. Kent.

Riverside Station; coast village in East Providence .... Providence.

Robin; hill in southern part of Providence on shore of Providence River; altitude, 80 feet.............................. Providence.

Rock; hill in northern part of Scituate....................... Burrillville.

Rock; hill in Coventry; elevation, 433 feet................... Kent.

Rock; island in upper part of Narragansett Bay.............. Providence.

Rock; point on south coast of South Kingstown .... Charlestown.

Rockland; village in Scituate .... Burrillville.

Rockville; village in western part of Hopkinton .... Moosup.

Rocky Brook; village in South Kingstown................... Charlestown.

Rocky; hill in northern part of Cranston; altitude, 183 feet... Providence.

Names of sheets.

Rocky; point projecting into Narragansett Bay from town of Warwick .... Narragansett Bay.

Rocky Point; village and railroad station on Warwick R. R., in Warwick .... Narragansett Bay.

Roger Williams Park; pleasure ground of the city of Providence, situated near its southern boundary.................. Providence.

Rome; point projecting from North Kingstown into Narragansett Bay.. Narragansett Bay.

Rose; hill in South Kingstown, Washington County; elevation, 240 feet... Newport.

Rose; island in southern part of Narragansett Bay .... Newport.

Round; pond (salt) near coast of Little Compton .... Sakonnet.

Round; pond in western part of Burrillville.................... Putman.

Round; swamp and point on Conanicut Island .... Narragansett Bay.

Rounds; hill on line between Scituate and Foster; altitude, 620 feet.. Burrillville.

Round Rocks; hill in Johnston.................................. Burrillville.

Round Top; village in Burrillville.............................. Burrillville.

Rumford; village in northern part of East Providence .... Providence.

Rumstick Neck; projection on south coast of Barrington, into Narragansett Bay.. Narragansett Bay.

Runnins; river flowing into Narragansett Bay and forming part of eastern boundary of State and of the town of East Providence... Providence.

Rush; brook tributary to Pawtuxet River...................... Burrillville.

Sabin; point projecting from East Providence into head of Narragansett Bay .... Providence.

Sachuest; beach on coast of Middletown..................... { Sakonnet.
 Newport.

Sachuest; point, the most southern point of Middletown at mouth of Sakonnet River................................... Sakonnet.

Sachuest Neck; peninsula projecting from Middletown at mouth of Sakonnet River.. Sakonnet.

Sakonnet; point, the most southern extremity of Little Compton. Sakonnet.

Sakonnet; river, an arm of Narragansett Bay, which connects { Sakonnet.
 Mount Hope Bay with it. { Fall River.

Sand; point projecting into Narragansett Bay from Prudence Island .... Narragansett Bay.

Sand; point on coast of Conanicut Island .... Narragansett Bay.

Sand; point projecting into Narragansett Bay from the town of Warwick .... Narragansett Bay.

Sand; pond in town of Warwick............................. Narragansett Bay.

Sands; pond on Block Island .... Block Island.

Sand Hill; cove in south coast of South Kingstown .... Newport.

Sandy; point on south shore of Greenwich Bay in town of Warwick .... Narragansett Bay.

Sandy; point forming outer end of Napatree Beach in Westerly. Stonington.

Sandy; point projecting from Portsmouth into Sakonnet River. Fall River.

Sandy; point on north end of Block Island; area 10·5 square miles .... Block Island.

Sapowet; point projecting from Tiverton into Sakonnet River. Fall River.

Sassafras; point projecting from southern part of Providence into Providence River .... Providence.

Sauga; point projecting from North Kingstown into Narragansett Bay .... Narragansett Bay.

Names of sheets.

Saugatuckett; river flowing into the Atlantic through Point Judith Pond in South Kingstown........................... Newport.

Saunderstown; coast village in southeast part of North Kingstown .... Narragansett Bay.

Saundersville; village in Scituate.............................. Burrillville.

Sawmill; hill in eastern part of Coventry; altitude, 226 feet... Kent.

Saxonville; village in Burrillville............................. Burrillville.

Sayles; hill in North Smithfield; altitude, 440 feet............. Burrillville.

Sayles Bleachery; village in Lincoln .... Providence.

Saylesville; village in Lincoln.................................. Providence.

School House; pond in central part of Charlestown............ Charlestown.

Scituate; town in Providence County; area, 52·3 square miles. { Burrillville. / Kent.

Scott; brook tributary to Blackstone River in Cumberland...... Providence.

Scott; pond in Lincoln... Providence.

Seal; island off southern point of Bristol Neck .... Fall River.

Seekonk; river tributary to Providence River, flowing through Pawtucket and forming boundary between Providence and East Providence, at head of Narragansett Bay............... Providence.

Shannock; hill in Richmond; altitude, 280 feet................ Charlestown.

Shannock; village in Richmond................................. Charlestown.

Shawomet Beach; village and railroad station on Warwick R. R. in Warwick.. Narragansett Bay.

Sheep; point on coast of Newport............................... Newport.

Sheep Pen; cove, a part of Narragansett Bay entering Prudence Island .... Narragansett Bay.

Sherman; hill in western part of North Kingstown; altitude, 292 feet.. Kent.

Sherman; island in Sakonnet River............................ Fall River.

Sherman Station; coast village in East Providence............ Providence.

Shippee; brook tributary to Pawtuxet River, in Foster........ Burrillville.

Shrub; hill in northern part of Exeter .... Kent.

Shumunkanug; hill in western part of Charlestown; altitude, 223 feet .... Charlestown.

Silver; lake in South Kingstown............................... Newport.

Silver Hook; railway station in Warwick .... Providence.

Silver Lake; village in Johnston .... Providence.

Silver Spring Station; coast village in East Providence .... Providence.

Simmonsville; village in Johnston............................. Burrillville.

Sin and Flesh; brook tributary to Sakonnet River, in town of Tiverton.. Fall River.

Sky High; hill in Providence; elevation 140 feet............... Providence.

Slack; reservoir in Smithfield and Johnston; elevation, 269 feet. Burrillville.

Slate; hill in Portsmouth; elevation, 260 feet .... Narragansett Bay.

Slatersville; village in northern part of North Smithfield ..... { Blackstone. / Burrillville.

Slocumville; village in North Kingstown .... Kent.

Smith; beach on coast of Middletown near mouth of Sakonnet River .... Sakonnet.

Smith; cove, a part of Warren River entering Barrington...... Narragansett Bay.

Smith and Sayles; reservoir in Glocester; elevation, 426 feet... Burrillville.

Smithfield; town in Providence County; area, 27·1 square miles. { Burrillville. / Providence.

Smithfield Station; village in Smithfield...................... Burrillville.

Names of sheets.

Skunk; hill in northeastern part of Hopkinton; altitude, 322 feet .... Kent.
Snake; hill in Glocester; elevation, 440 feet..................... Burrillville.
Snake; hill in Burrillville; altitude, 533 feet................... Burrillville.
Snake Den; hill in Johnston; elevation, 380 feet .... Burrillville.
Sneech; brook tributary to Blackstone River in Cumberland... Providence.
Sneech; pond in Cumberland.................................... Providence.
Sockanosset; reservoir, a small artificial pond in Cranston .... Providence.
Sockanosset; village in Cranston on Providence R. R.......... Providence.
Sodom; brook tributary to Queen River in Exeter............. Kent.
South Foster; village in Foster................................ Burrillville.
South Kingstown; seaboard town in southeastern portion of Washington County; area, 77·9 square miles. } Kent. Charlestown. Newport.
South Scituate; village in Scituate............................ Burrillville.
Southeast; point on coast of Block Island...................... Block Island.
Southwest; point projecting from Hog Island into Narragansett Bay... Narragansett Bay.
Southwest; point on east coast of Conanicut Island, projecting into Narragansett Bay .... Newport.
Southwest; point on coast of Block Island.................... Block Island.
Spar; island in Mount Hope Bay .... Fall River.
Spectacle; island in Sakonnet River .... Fall River.
Spectacle; pond in northern part of Cranston.................. Providence.
Spencer; hill in Warwick; elevation, 348 feet .... Narragansett Bay.
Spink Neck; island in Allen Harbor, North Kingstown .... Narragansett Bay.
Spragueville; a village in Smithfield........................... Burrillville.
Spring Green; pond in town of Warwick...................... Narragansett Bay.
Spring Grove; village in Glocester............................. Burrillville.
Spring Grove; village and railroad station on Warwick R. R. in Warwick .... Narragansett Bay.
Spruce; brook tributary to Pawtuxet River .... Burrillville.
Squantum; coast village in East Providence .... Providence.
Squepaug; village in South Kingstown........................ Kent.
Stafford; pond in northern part of Tiverton..................... Fall River.
Starve Goat; island in Narragansett Bay near its head........ Providence.
Steere; hill in Glocester; elevation, 580 feet .... Burrillville.
Stillwater; village in Smithfield .... Burrillville.
Stump; hill in Lincoln; altitude, 304 feet..................... Providence.
Sucker; brook in Burrillville and Glocester tributary to Chepachet River... Burrillville.
Sucker; pond in Burrillville; elevation, 437 feet............... Burrillville.
Sugarloaf; hill in South Kingstown........................... Charlestown.
Summit; village in Coventry................................... Kent.
Swamp; brook tributary to Pawtuxet River.................... Burrillville.
Taney; brook in Richmond..................................... Charlestown.
Tarkiln Station; village in Burrillville........................ Burrillville.
Tefft; hill in northern part of Richmond; altitude, 461 feet..... Kent.
Tefft; hill in South Kingstown; altitude, 255 feet .... Charlestown.
Ten Mile; river tributary to Seekonk River, which forms a portion of eastern boundary of the State and of the town of East Providence... Providence.
Thirty Acre; pond in South Kingstown.......... .... Charlestown.
Thornton; village in southern part of Johnston................ Providence.

Names of sheets.

Tiogue; reservoir in eastern part of Coventry .... Kent.

Tippecan; pond on boundary between Greenwich and Exeter; altitude, 375 feet .... Moosup.

Tiverton; town in Newport County; area, 31.8 square miles .... Fall River.

Tiverton; village, in Tiverton .... Fall River.

Tiverton Four Corners; village in Tiverton .... Fall River.

Tom Mount; hill in Exeter; altitude 428 feet .... Kent.

Tomaquang; brook tributary to Pawcatuck River in Hopkinton. Stonington.

Tommy; island in Sakonnet River .... Fall River.

Tourtellot; hill in Glocester; elevation, 684 feet .... Burrillville.

Tower; hill, having the form of a long ridge with a bluff face to the east in South Kingstown; elevation, 178 feet .... Newport.

Toweset; point projecting from southern part of Warren into Mount Hope Bay .... Fall River.

Town; tidal pond in northern part of Portsmouth .... Fall River.

Truns; pond (salt) upon Block Island .... Block Island.

Truston; pond (salt) on coast of South Kingstown .... Charlestown.

Tucker; pond in South Kingstown; elevation, 97 feet .... Charlestown.

Tunipus; pond on coast of Little Compton .... Sakonnet.

Tunipus; beach on coast of Little Compton .... Sakonnet.

Tunk; hill in southern part of Scituate; altitude, 546 feet ...... Burrillville.

Tuscatucket; river in town of Warwick, flowing into Narragansett Bay .... Narragansett Bay.

Twin; islands in Seekonk River just above its mouth .... Providence.

Upper; pond forming the northern portion of Point Judith Pond. Newport.

Usher; cove extending from Bristol Harbor in town of Bristol. Narragansett Bay.

Usquepaug; river tributary to Charles River in Richmond...... Charlestown.

Valley Falls; village in southern part of Cumberland.......... Providence.

Vernon, village in southern part of Foster..................... Kent.

Vue de l'eau; coast village in East Providence................. Providence.

Wakefield; pond in western part of Burrillville; height, 535 feet .... Putnam.

Wakefield; village in South Kingstown...................... { Charlestown. Newport.

Walcott; fort on Goat Island at entrance to Newport Harbor.. Newport.

Wallum; pond in western part of Burrillville; height, 575 feet.. Putnam.

Wanskuck; village in Providence............................... Providence.

Warren; point on coast of Little Compton..................... Sakonnet.

Warren; river heading in Massachusetts and flowing between towns of Warren and Barrington into Narragansett Bay. { Providence. Narragansett Bay.

Warren; town in northeastern part of Bristol County; area, 5·9 square miles. { Fall River. Kent. Narragansett Bay.

Warren; principal village in town of same name in Bristol County at junction of Providence, Warren and Bristol, and Warren and Fall River railroads....................................... Narragansett Bay.

Warren Neck; projection of land into Mount Hope Bay mainly within town of Warren.. Fall River.

Warwick; pond in town of Warwick............................ Narragansett Bay.

Warwick; town in Kent County; area, 44·2 square miles....... { Narragansett Bay. Providence.

Warwick; village and railroad station on Warwick R. R. in Warwick .... Narragansett Bay.

Names of sheets.

Warwick Neck; peninsula projecting into Narragansett Bay, part of the town of Warwick .... Narragansett Bay.

Wash; pond of salt water in southern part of Block Island .... Block Island.

Wash; pond in southern part of South Kingstown .... Charlestown.

Washington; village in Coventry .... Kent.

Watchaug; pond in southwestern part of Charlestown .... Charlestown.

Watchemoket; cove projecting into East Providence from Providence River .... Providence.

Watch Hill; seashore village on coast of Westerly .... Stonington.

Watch Hill; point near the village of same name in Westerly .. Stonington.

Watch Hill; pond or salt lagoon in south part of Westerly .... Stonington.

Westerly; village in town of same name situated on Pawcatuck River and New York, Providence and Boston R. R .... Stonington.

White; brook in Richmond .... Charlestown.

White; pond in southern part of South Kingstown .... Charlestown.

White Rock; village in west part of Westerly .... Stonington.

Whortleberry; hill in North Smithfield; altitude, 460 feet..... Burrillville.

Wickaboxet; pond in western part of Greenwich; elevation, 314 feet... Moosup.

Wickford; cove, a part of Narragansett Bay entering North Kingstown... Narragansett Bay.

Wickford; village on coast of North Kingstown .... Narragansett Bay.

Wickford Junction; village and railway station in North Kingstown .... Narragansett Bay.

Wilbur; hill in Richmond; altitude, 300 feet .... Charlestown.

Wild Goose; point projecting from North Kingstown into Narragansett Bay.. Narragansett Bay.

Wilson; reservoir in Burrillville; elevation, 446 feet........... Burrillville.

Waterman; reservoir in Smithfield and Glocester; elevation, 438 feet... Burrillville.

Wayland Station; station in Cranston on New York and New England R. R .... Providence.

Weaver; hill in southern part of Coventry; elevation, 601 feet.. Kent.

Weeks; hill in Coventry; altitude, 600 feet.................... Kent.

Wesquage; pond of salt water near east coast of South Kingstown .... Newport.

West; island off coast of Little Compton .... Sakonnet.

West Glocester; village in western part of Glocester.......... Putnam.

West Greenville; village in Smithfield .... Burrillville.

West Greenwich; town in Kent County .... Kent.

West Greenwich Center; village in western part of Greenwich .... Moosup.

West Kingstown; village in South Kingstown, on Providence R. R .... Charlestown.

West Meadow; brook in southern part of Foster .... Burrillville.

Westconnaug; reservoir in southeastern part of Foster; elevation, 450 feet .... Burrillville.

Westerly; town in southwest part of Washington County; area, 31·1 square miles .... Charlestown.

Wincheck; pond in western part of Hopkinton; height, 315 feet.. Moosup.

Wind Mill; hill on boundary between Pawtucket, North Providence, and Providence: altitude, 180 feet................... Providence.

Windmill; hill in northwest part of Little Compton; altitude, 140 feet... Fall River.

Names of sheets.

Wionkhiege; hill in Smithfield; elevation 557 feet.............. Burrillville.

Wolf Rock; group of hills in southeastern part of Exeter; altitude, 302 feet ....·................................. Kent.

Worden; pond in South Kingstown, drained by Charles River; elevation, 94 feet... Charlestown.

Wood; river tributary to Pawcatuck River, forming boundary between Richmond and Hopkinton.......................... Charlestown.

Wood River Junction; village in Richmond.................... Charlestown.

Woods Castle; point on coast of Middletown, extending into { Sakonnet. Sakonnet River.   { Fall River.

Woodlawn; village in Pawtucket.............................. Providence.

Woodville; village in Hopkinton............................. Charlestown.

Woodville; village in North Providence....................... Providence.

Woody; hill in Exeter; altitude, 427 feet .... Kent.

Woonasquatucket; branch of Providence River, forming boundary between Providence, North Providence, and Johnston .... Providence.

Woonsocket; town in northern part of Providence County; { Franklin. { Blackstone. area, 8·4 square miles.   { Burrillville. { Providence.

Woonsocket; hill in North Smithfield; altitude, 588 feet...... Burrillville.

Wyoming; village in western part of Richmond............... Kent.

Yawgoag; pond in western part of Hopkinton; height, 329 feet. Moosup.

Yawgoo; pond in northern part of South Kingstown; elevation, 120 feet.. Kent.

Yawker; hill in southwestern part of Exeter; altitude, 315 feet. Kent.

○

www.ingramcontent.com/pod-product-compliance
Lightning Source LLC
Chambersburg PA
CBHW072209270326
41930CB00011B/2586